His Pearl I Am

...a work in progress

Sharon Fox

Pearl Publishing

Copyright © 2014 Pearl Publishing

All rights reserved.

ISBN: 0-692-31596-9

ISBN-13: 978-0-692-31596-5

Author's Photography by Eddie Brannon

Cover Photo: Gino Santa Maria, www.shutterfree.com

Cover Design by Donna Osborn Clark, CreationByDonna.com

Interior Layout by Glenda Wallace, www.pinkkisspublishing.com

I am so thankful for all the life lessons, prayers, and inspirations that were necessary for the writing of this book. Without knowing who God is and the power in the name of Jesus, I would have never been able to survive the many obstacles that strengthened my faith over the years. For this reason, I dedicate this book to the one person who made such a great impact on my life and encouraged me to hold on to the hand of the Lord.

This dedication is to my father, Rev. Garner Ray Skelton. I am so grateful to God for allowing him to be the most important part of my life when I needed a loving father, friend, counselor, and teacher. After losing him in February 2012, his lessons and words of wisdom helped to guide me even closer to God. Those great lessons I have passed on to my children, grandchildren, and now to you.

I love you Daddy.

Acknowledgments

To my Pastors, Bill and Debbie Bryan, Andrew and Tara Bryan, and Darrell Young: Thank you for your love, support and encouragement for the past two years. There were so many moments that I didn't have the courage to move forward with writing this book. Your teaching and examples of dedication have given me the inspiration I needed to answer this call from God. I will always honor you and respect you for the behind the scenes work you do when no one is looking. I am honored to call you Pastors.

To Evangelist David Copeland: Thank you for speaking a word into my life that will always fuel me to keep doing what I do for the Lord. I admire what you do in the darkest parts of the world for the glory of God. Thanks for all your encouraging words for the past 15 months. I am honored to call you Brother.

To Evangelist Anthony Cole: Thank you for looking past my smile and speaking life directly into my Spirit. My life will never be the same! I pray that God will bless you exceedingly and abundantly more than you may ask or think. I am honored to call you Friend.

To Pastor Tony Hagan: You'll never know the power of a word spoken to me through you in July 2013. Those words caused my life to be shaken into place. I will always honor you for your obedient walk with God. May you continue to grow as your ministry expands to touch thousands of lives. I am honored to call you a model of Jesus in my life.

To Evangelist Eusherla Pitts: Thank you for being such a strong, beautiful woman of God. You have shown so much strength when I knew you were weak. I pray God's best blessings will overtake you. I love you from the bottom of my heart for being a truly virtuous woman of God.

This book has been in my heart since 2011. The year of 2012 was extremely hard for me after losing my father. I needed Spiritual guidance in order to overcome the things that were going on in my life during that time. I owe all glory to God for bringing these special people into my life. Through their teaching, prophetic words, and down to earth ministries that reach into the world to help heal so many hurting souls, I was equipped to go forth to answer my calling. I pray that God will allow me to bless you all as much as you've blessed me. Contact information for these ministries are at the end of this book. I encourage you to contact them if you need Spiritual guidance.

Contents

PREFACE 1
INTRODUCTION 3
THE ROAD TO SALVATION 7
THE GROWING PROCESS 13
1 ~ BEAUTY OF WORSHIP 17
2 ~ FORGIVING 23
3 ~ IN THE POTTER'S HAND 29
4 ~ MY BEAUTIFUL MESS 35
5 ~ CHANGE 41
6 ~ CHOICES 47
7 ~ THE VOICE OF GOD 53
8 ~ YOUR DIVINE PURPOSE 59
9 ~ HE KEEPS HIS PROMISES 65
10 ~ WAKE UP YOUR DEAD DREAMS 71
11 ~ ACCOUNTABILITY 77
12 ~ MY WEAKNESS, HIS STRENGTH 83
13 ~ THE COMPANY YOU KEEP 89
14 ~ NEVER ALONE 95
15 ~ SELF IMAGE 101
16 ~ FAITH REVEALED 107
17 ~ PURSUIT OF PERFECTION 113
18 ~ FEAR OF REJECTION 119
19 ~ TEMPORARY PLEASURES 125
20 ~ EARTHLY TREASURES 131
21 ~ FROM ADDICTION TO DEVOTION 137
22 ~ DEALING WITH GUILT 143
23 ~ CHOOSE LIFE 149
24 ~ GRIEF 155
25 ~ OVERLOOKED AND UNAPPRECIATED 161
26 ~ SCARS OF LIFE 167
27 ~ INFERTILITY: THE MISSING PIECE 173
28 ~ G.I.C.U 179
29 ~ PRISON OF TEMPTATION 185

30 ~ PRIDE	191
31 ~ SECRETS	197
32 ~ DEPRESSION	203
33 ~ INTEGRITY	209
34 ~ RESPECT	215
35 ~ WHAT MY FRUIT LOOKS LIKE	221
36 ~ PATIENCE	227
37 ~ TEMPER, TEMPER	233
38 ~ THE POWER OF LUST	239
39 ~ GREED	245
40 ~ JEALOUSY	251
41 ~ THE TONGUE	257
42 ~ SPIRITUAL DANGER	263
43 ~ HOMELESS	269
44 ~ WHAT DO YOU BELIEVE?	275
45 ~ UNCONDITIONAL LOVE	281
46 ~ MY PROVIDER	287
47 ~ MORE THAN A CONQUEROR	293
48 ~ WHAT IS SUCCESS?	299
49 ~ ALL FOR HIS GLORY	305
50 ~ BLESSINGS IN GIVING BACK	311
51 ~ WORTH IT ALL	317
52 ~ HIS PEARL I AM	323
CONCLUSION	329
MINISTRY ACKNOWLEDGMENTS	331
ABOUT THE AUTHOR	333

PREFACE

A work in progress. You are very valuable and precious to God. This value does not diminish according to your background, race, financial status, or how others may judge you. God created you to be different from anyone else and He loves you unconditionally.

This book is a weekly devotional designed to guide you through a whole year of learning just how much you mean to Him. It will challenge you to be all you can be, to find strength where you are weak, and to allow each day to be a beautiful, new adventure in your life.

You will find it to be very personal for your own life. The journal section is between you and God. So much prayer and studying has gone into developing this book to be the Life Coach you need to learn your value to the world and to the Father.

If you have decided to live your best life, discover your true self, and let the power of God bring light to all your dark places, then prepare to dedicate the next fifty-two weeks to earnestly seeking the beautiful life that you were created to live.

God created pearls, and you are one of them. Find out how your life compares to the precious pearl as you enjoy divine moments each day in a relationship with your Creator.

INTRODUCTION

Have you ever read about the parable involving "the pearl of great price" in Matthew 13:44-46 or about the "twelve gates of pearls" of the coming new heavenly Jerusalem in Revelation 21:21? Have you ever wondered why God would use a pearl as the main component of this parable to symbolize the Kingdom of God? Have you ever wondered why the entrances into the headquarters of the new heavens and new earth known as the "twelve gates" will be made of pearls? You would think they would be made of diamonds, solid gold, or some other gem seemingly of more value.

Well, I believe the answer lies in the unique way that God designed the formation of pearls. I know most of you would say, "But pearls come from oysters." Yes, they do. But there is so much more to the wonderful and exquisite details of the making of a pearl that deserves our attention.

First of all, pearls are unique to the world of gems because they are the only ones that are individually formed from a living organism. Other gems, like diamonds or rubies for example, must be found within the earth, mined, and cut and shaped into sizes and shapes according to consumer preferences.

On the other hand, pearls are formed one at a time when a foreign particle or parasite becomes lodged in the soft tissue of an oyster. The oyster identifies it as an intruder, and tries to isolate it from spreading. To relieve the irritation, the oyster coats the parasite with a secretion called nacre. This nacre is actually the substance that forms pearls. The oyster will form several layers of this substance which continues to build up over time. Depending on how long the parasite remains in the oyster, these layers accumulate to determine the size and shape of each pearl.

Despite the uniqueness, you might still wonder why God would use pearls in these two biblical instances to describe items of such great value. That answer is found in history.

Today, pearls are cultured. A single irritant is manually inserted into millions of oysters at pearl farms around the world and then harvested later.

Even with modern technology, only about half of these oysters will produce a pearl and only about 25% of those will be marketable to sell. Ultimately, only about 5% of the original crop of nucleated oysters will produce high-quality pearls. You see, there is a lot of work involved in the pearl culturing business without a very high payoff. And this is after years and years of "going through the process".

Pearls are documented as far back as the 5th century B.C. in Roman and Egyptian cultures. They were called the "Queen of Gems" and reserved for the wealthy and powerful. Why? Because pearl culturing didn't come about until the 20th century. Therefore, a natural pearl was only found in about one out of every 10,000 oysters. In order to make a single necklace, you'd have to go through about 500,000 oysters! This is why pearls were rare and special treasures. To top it all off, diving for pearls was very dangerous. Most pearl oysters live several feet into the ocean and in those ancient days, there was no scuba diving gear. They had to risk their lives confronting jellyfish, sharks, and other sea creatures while searching for them.

This is why the Romans valued pearls so greatly. They viewed them as a symbol of wealth and status in society. Only those deemed worthy enough could even wear them. Now can you see why God would use this beautiful, exquisitely made gem for such high purposes?

Sometimes it takes a little more effort to scratch the surface of a topic to understand what lies beneath the layers. You, my friend, are a pearl in the eyes of God. A work in progress. You may have been affected by parasites which are unwelcome circumstances in your life. The years of protecting yourself from the pain, hiding behind a smile, holding back the tears, and building up walls were all layers of nacre that created the beautiful pearl that you are today.

Hold your head up and know that you, yes you, are very valuable and beautiful in the eyes of God. Devote the next 52 weeks to this weekly devotion and allow Him to show you just how much He loves you. And after your eyes and heart are opened to this revelation, please tell someone else.

THE ROAD TO SALVATION

If you place your hand over your heart right now, you'll feel a precious gift from God. That heartbeat is all that stands between you and your eternal life in heaven or hell. Stop and think about that for a moment. If you were to die today, do you know for sure where you'd be spending your eternal life? If you are not sure about the answer to that question, then this is a great time to start your journey on the road to salvation.

You might say: I'm really a "good" person. Isn't that good enough to make it into heaven?

God's word says in Romans 3:23 that "all have sinned and fallen short of the glory of God." Then Romans 3:10 tells us that "There is none righteous, no, not one." Finally, Romans 5:12 reminds us that "Therefore, just as through one man (Adam) sin entered the world, and death through sin, and thus death spread to all men, because all sinned."

God is our Creator. He is light and in Him is no darkness at all. (1 John 1:5)

There are laws for His creation to obey. The first of these laws are the Ten Commandments. Even though you may be a good person compared to most of the people you know, how do you think you measure up against God's law? Even if you've only told a "little white lie", you are still a liar. James 2:10 tells us "For whoever keeps the whole law and yet stumbles at just one point is guilty of breaking all of it."

You might say: Sin can't really be that big of a deal. If it is...what hope do I have?

I'm so glad you asked. Romans 6:23 tells us "The wages of sin is death, but the gift of God is eternal life in Christ Jesus our Lord."

You see my friend, disobedience to an infinite and eternal God deserves an infinite and eternal consequence. Not only has God given us written laws, He has also written words in our hearts. This is also called your "conscience". His word is the Bible. Any good judge will never let the guilty go free. The legal system is designed to never let the criminals go without punishment. Neither will our God allow a sinful man to go unpunished. But there is hope. Even in sin, God provided a way of escape by sending His only son, Jesus Christ, to die in our place. All you must do is accept Him into your heart and your sins will be pardoned.

You might say: I have disappointed God so much, how could Jesus willingly die for me?

Your answers are all in the Word of God. Romans 5:8 says, "But God demonstrates His own love toward us, in that while we were still sinners, Christ died for us." Then, John 3:16 lets us know that "God so loved the world that He gave His only begotten Son, that whosoever believes in Him should not perish but have everlasting life." Jesus even spoke up for you and all sinners while He was on the cross. Luke 23:34 says, "While He died on the cross, He was mocked and spit upon, and cursed. Yet Jesus cried out, Father forgive them for they know not what they do."

Jesus died in your place, a horrible death. His love abounded even after knowing every evil word you'd say, every sinful act you'd commit, and every devilish thought you'd ever have. He really does love you unconditionally, even when you are at your lowest point in life.

Your question now may be: Then how can I possibly be saved?

The Bible says in Romans 10:9-10 that "If you confess with your mouth the Lord Jesus and believe in your heart that God raised Him from the dead, you will be saved. For with the heart one believes unto righteousness, and with the mouth confession is made unto salvation."

My dear friend, you will never be saved by doing good deeds, treating people kindly, or having good intentions. Only God can give you salvation. Ephesians 2:8-9 says, "For by grace have you been saved by faith. And that, not of yourselves. It is the gift of God, not of works. Lest any man should boast."

You see, we can only be saved by confessing our sins and having faith in Jesus, who died on the cross. We must surrender our lives to His lordship and place Him in charge of our lives because we now belong to Him.

You might ask: How do I know for sure that God heard my prayer and accepted me?

You can be assured through the word of God. Romans 10:13 says, "Whoever calls on the name of the Lord shall be saved." In John 1:12, God promises that "to all who received Him, to those who believed in His name, he gave the right to become children of God."

Yes, God does hear and accept all who come to Him and put their faith in Him. Once you accept Jesus as your Savior, believe in your heart that He is the living Son of God who died and was raised again from the dead, and is now preparing a place for you in heaven, you are SAVED! If you'd like to accept Jesus as your savior right now, say this prayer:

> **Dear Heavenly Father, I come to you in the precious name of Jesus. I am a sinner and I stand in need of your forgiveness for the way I have lived my life. I believe that your only son, Jesus Christ, shed His precious blood on the cross at Calvary and died for remission of my sins. You said in your word, Romans 10:9-10, that if I confess your son Jesus as my Lord and Savior and believe in my heart that He was raised from the dead for my salvation, I shall be saved.**
>
> **Right now, I confess Jesus as the Lord of my soul. With all my heart, I believe that with your power, He was raised from the dead. I accept Jesus as my own personal Savior, and according to the word I am now saved. Thank you for your grace and mercy which has saved me from my sins. Thank you for the Holy Spirit that will always lead and guide me to repentance. Transform my life so that I may bring glory to you alone.**
>
> **Thank you for giving me a new life, a clean heart, and eternal life with you. In Jesus' precious name, Amen.**

Your last question may be: Now that I am saved, what do I do now?

Well, my dear Sister or Brother, it's now time to walk in faith. The word of God says in Romans 10:17 "So then faith cometh by hearing, and hearing by the word of God."

Your journey as a child of God has just begun. Don't take your salvation for granted. You must build a close relationship with Father God by spending time with Him daily. The way to do this is to begin your day in prayer and read His word. Make this a part of your daily life. Get up a few minutes earlier to set aside this time for Him. Take some time mid-day to do the same. And please remember to thank Him before going to sleep. He loves you dearly, and just like any person you love - He wants to have communication with you.

You must also find fellowship with other believers in a church that teaches and preaches about the love of Jesus. In addition to these two things, you must tell others that you have accepted Jesus as your savior. Share His love with others. There will be many opportunities for you to tell others about the love of God and how He changed your life for the better.

THE GROWING PROCESS

"I am the true vine, and my Father is the gardener. He cuts off every branch in me that bears no fruit, while every branch that does bear fruit He prunes so that it will be even more fruitful. You are already clean because of the word I have spoken to you. Remain in me, as I also remain in you. No branch can bear fruit by itself; it must remain in the vine. Neither can you bear fruit unless you remain in me." ~John 15:1-4 (NIV)

Once you accept Jesus into your life as Lord and Savior, it is very important that you continue to grow. When we apply this scripture to our lives, we must see Father God as the gardener, Jesus as the vine, and we are the branches. The vine is the sustenance of life for the branches, and it is vital for those branches to stay connected to the vine in order to live and bear fruit.

What is this fruit? It is living according to the word of God and allowing this new life to be a light for others to find their way to Him as well. You are now a disciple, a disciplined follower of Jesus. When others look at you, they see the God inside of you. That's why it is very important for you to stay attached to the vine. This is why your daily communication with Him is so important. There is no way you can stay attached to someone if you never take time to talk to them.

This is not to say that you will always live a perfect life, spotless before God. We all make mistakes in our weakness, but this is why your relationship with Him is so important. You can always go to Him, repent, and ask for forgiveness. This is where the pruning process comes into play. When you are bearing fruit - witnessing to others and living according to God's word - the Lord will prune away things from your life so that you will be able to bear even more fruit. Believe me, you'd much rather go through a pruning process than to be a withered up branch that produces no fruit. The gardener burns all those dead, dry branches!

Be a healthy, nourished branch. Stay connected to the vine. Produce good fruit for the Kingdom. You are so precious to the family of God and you will be able to touch people that others may never be able to touch. There are souls depending on you to show them the way to salvation. You weren't saved just to have a seat in heaven, you are now a light for someone else's dark path. Live your life knowing that someone is watching you. There is an old saying that says, "You are the only bible some people will ever read." Live your life accordingly. Pray for the guidance of the Holy Spirit in your life daily.

I pray that this book will help you along your walk with Jesus. There are so many wonderful things that God wants to show you about His faithfulness. He loves you more than you could ever imagine. As the days, months, and years go by you will understand more about how your life compares with the beautiful pearl.

During the next fifty-two weeks, we will touch on several topics. Some of which will be very sensitive to you, some will be enlightening, and some will be humorous. All in all, this will be a very interesting year for you. Life has a way of delivering to your doorstep so many unexpected packages like joy, sadness, grief, love, broken hearts, rejection, promotion, etc.

I encourage you to seriously devote yourself to doing the work that is necessary in order to find your inner pearl. God will bring out what He placed within you, if you allow Him to take you through the process.

In order for this book to be most productive in your life, I suggest you begin and end every day with prayer. Even though this is a weekly devotion, I don't want you to only spend time with Father God once a week. It is imperative that you build a strong relationship with Him. You don't have to pray like a pastor to touch His heart. All you have to do is be sincere and talk to Him from your heart. He already knows all about you anyway. He loves you and wants to hear how much you love Him!

I am so honored to have this opportunity to share the things that God has placed in my heart with you. I am grateful to be called by Him to do this work for you and with you. Take my hand as we begin this journey together.

> *"The Lord bless you and keep you;*
> *The Lord make His face shine upon you,*
> *And be gracious to you;*
> *The Lord lift up His countenance upon you,*
> *And give you peace."*

Numbers 6:24-26 (NKJV)

1 ~ BEAUTY OF WORSHIP

"The heavens declare the glory of God; the skies proclaim the work of His hands. Day after day they pour forth speech; night after night they reveal knowledge. They have no speech, they use no words; no sound is heard from them. Yet their voice goes out into all the earth, their words to the end of the world." (Psalms 19:1-4)

This is such an amazing scripture. Looking into the skies and meditating on this word amazes me and leaves me in awe of just how wonderful our God is. When you declare the glory of God, something amazing happens. Worship is the perfect medicine for a broken heart. There is a healing power in sincere worship. The nature of worship is not self centered, it's God centered. All attention is on Him. When you lavish Him with love from a pure heart and clean hands, you will experience His presence. The word tells us in Psalms 16:11 that in His presence is fullness of joy.

I want you to find some time each day, preferably early in the morning before you begin your day, to meditate on His goodness, the beauty of His creation, and the mercy that only He can give every day. As you allow this scripture to sink down into your inner being, I pray that you will be humbled by His majesty. As you come closer to Him, you will find yourself refreshed and renewed daily in His presence. Forget all about yourself and indulge into His whole being. Soon you will become less focused on your problems and will discover His miraculous hand removing them one by one.

Remember, it's all about Him and never about you. Worship is a holy time set aside for you to have intimacy with your Creator. Finding that special quiet place is very important. Some people find their special place walking near the water. Some find it easier to be alone with Him walking in the park. No matter where you choose to be alone with Him, be sure to value that time and place.

The more you worship Him, the closer you will get to His heart. The closer you get to His heart, the more your life will change. No matter how many relationships you ever have, there will never be one like yours with Father God. I guarantee that once you make that divine connection with Him, you will not want it to be broken.

Worship Him in spirit and in truth. He knows your heart, your inner thoughts, your hurts, your past, your future, and your circumstance. Why not give Him the adoration that only He deserves? He loves you unconditionally. Lift Him up every day. Watch how He gives you an unexplainable joy!

MY PRAYER: WEEK 1

Father God, I worship you for all that you are to me. You are so magnificent, I cannot praise you enough. Thank you for giving me grace and mercy each and every day of my life. I desire to seek your presence and lay before you because only you deserve my worship and my praise. I give my all to you, casting my cares at your feet. Be with me in everything I do. Make me the worshipper who will bring glory and honor to your name. Never let me go and never take your spirit from me. In Jesus name, amen.

MY SCRIPTURE

Psalms 145 (Entire chapter)

Read this text at least once each day, preferably upon waking and before going to bed.

MY CHALLENGE: WEEK 1

This week's challenge may be easy or it may be something new for you. I encourage you to continue this challenge beyond this week! Learning to worship God requires dedication. If you aren't serious about it, I suggest you pray and ask Him to give you a desire to do so.

Look at your daily schedule and choose a 15 minute period that is uninterrupted by anyone or anything. Find a special place where you can be alone to give Him all your attention. This may mean getting up 15 minutes earlier, going into a bathroom and locking the door, or even leaving the house to take a walk. However you do it, just do it. Take these 15 minutes to worship Him. This isn't a time to "ask" for anything, this is just time for you to recognize Him and remind Him of who He is to you and why.

Open your heart and allow His presence to overtake you. You may find yourself laughing, crying, singing, or all the above. Don't worry, His presence makes things happen like that.. Worship is the most important part of your Christian life. Learn to master it. After a month of doing this, it will become a very good habit. You will find that after doing this for only a few minutes at a time, you'll begin to worship for longer periods of time. God loves it, and you will too! Engage in His presence.

MY PERSONAL JOURNAL

WEEK 1

MY GOALS:

MY ACCOMPLISHMENTS:

2 ~ FORGIVING

"For if you forgive other people when they sin against you, your heavenly Father will also forgive you. But if you do not forgive others their sins, your Father will not forgive your sins." (Matthew 6:14-15)

Forgiveness is something that may be hard to deal with at times for all of us. I'm not talking about forgiving someone for stepping on your toe, spilling your glass, or breaking a window. The most difficult things to forgive are those deep wounds that may last a lifetime. Those harsh words spoken in rage that you never seem to forget that still haunt you today. The physical, sexual, or emotional abuse that you endured and you carried that hurt for years. The rejection, criticism, or embarrassment you held inside because it hurt too bad to discuss. All these things can cause you to never want to forgive the one(s) who did these things to you. But if you want God to forgive you, then you must forgive others.

True forgiveness is often misunderstood. Forgiveness is not making an excuse for the action. *"He only did it because he was drunk."* Forgiveness is not thinking that after so much time goes by, all will be forgotten and we can go on with our lives. And forgiveness does not necessarily mean you have to go face to face with the person and forgive them. God forgave us long before we were born, long before we actually asked for forgiveness (see 1 John 1:9). Sometimes confronting a person to forgive them will actually stir up even more resentment. In such cases, you need to take it to the Father and leave it there. Tell Him that you forgive that person for what they did and do not ever bring it up again. Now there will be times when face to face forgiveness is necessary. Your situation is unique, so pray and ask God about how to handle it. In any case, you must forgive.

How do you know for sure you have completely forgiven someone? You will find yourself praying for their good instead of secretly wishing bad things would happen to them. You will accept them as they are, knowing that only God can change their heart. Finally, you will feel total freedom! There is no greater feeling than the inner peace God gives you when you forgive others. When you release yourself from the bondage of that unforgiving spirit, you release the blessings of God to flow freely in your life. He wants to see you blessed and walking freely in a life of purpose so that you can be a blessing to others. Do you want to be forgiven? Then you must forgive others. You can do it. God loves you so much, He will give you the grace you need to do it because He wants to see you free in love.

MY PRAYER: WEEK 2

Father God, I just want to thank you for teaching me about forgiveness. Open my heart to forgive others the way You want to forgive me. Grant me grace and mercy as I forgive anyone who has done me wrong and/or caused me any physical, mental, or emotional pain. Give me the mind of Christ so that I will walk in Your divine will of love and forgiveness. I desire to be the person you created me to be. I claim my freedom from the bondage of an unforgiving heart right now, in Jesus name, amen.

MY SCRIPTURES

Ephesians 4:31-32
Read this scripture each morning and keep it in your heart.

Study: Genesis 50:16-21

MY CHALLENGE: WEEK 2

FORGIVING

This is a topic that we don't readily rush into with joy in our hearts. Remember that if you want to keep your relationship with God pure and clean, it is always good to make sure that you aren't holding any resentment or unforgiving feelings inside.

Your challenge this week is to make a list of people who you feel have wronged you, and you haven't truly forgiven them. Lay the list before God in prayer and <u>sincerely</u> forgive each one. Ask God to direct you from there. You may or may not have to face that person and verbally forgive them. Once you truly have forgiven them, you will experience a freedom like no other. Thank God for forgiving you because you have obeyed His word by forgiving others. Know that since you have erased all those things from your heart, God has erased them as well. You have no reason to hold on to the past. Let it all go and move forward. Congratulations! You are free!!

MY PERSONAL JOURNAL

WEEK 2

MY GOALS:

MY ACCOMPLISHMENTS:

3 ~ IN THE POTTER'S HAND

"Yet, O Lord, you are our Father. We are the clay, you are the potter; we are the works of your hand." (Isaiah 64:8)

Have you ever felt like you were being tossed and turned, flipped upside down, and squeezed until you just can't stand the pain? Imagine how wet clay feels on a potter's wheel. Slapped around, spun in circles over and over again while pressure is being applied in all the weakest places. That's exactly how you are in the hands of God.

He is in the process of making and molding you into the person He wants you to be. It's not easy. As a matter of fact, it's down- right painful at times. The Creator is shaping your character by the events and circumstances in your life. He is more concerned about your character than your comfort. It's natural for you to try to avoid pain and discomfort, but it's the very pain and discomfort that you try to avoid that builds the character of Jesus in your life.

Your character is built more by the trials you endure than by the blessings you receive. Your life as a Christian should be a mirror of Jesus. Not always beauty and grace, but survival and endurance should be what draws attention to the God in you. Others should see the hand of God in your life. The changes He has made in your life when they have witnessed the good, bad, and the ugly.

God doesn't expect you to come to Him in perfect condition. He has to "make" you into a vessel that He can use. Your condition is never too bad for God to use you. Just look in the bible and study about some of the people He used. The Samaritan Woman was divorced many times, Noah was a drunk, David was a murderer and adulterer, Elijah was suicidal, Moses had low self-esteem, Peter was a coward, Jacob was a deceiver, Samson was a womanizer, and even Rahab was a prostitute.

No, you aren't perfect, but you are a Child of the Living God. His grace covers you and that alone means that you, my dear, are wonderfully flawed. Jeremiah 18:4 says, *"But the pot he was shaping from the clay was marred (waste, damaged goods); so the potter formed it into another pot, shaping it as it seemed best to Him."*

Who cares if you're a "cracked pot" right now. God is not through with you yet. You are being shaped into a vessel, a masterpiece, that will bring honor and glory to the King. When it's all over and done, you will find the signature of the Maker engraved in your heart. So stay on the Potter's wheel. You can be a magnificent piece of work... if you withstand the process!

MY PRAYER: WEEK 3

Dear Heavenly Father, I come to you as a broken vessel. With you as my Potter, I know that I can be repaired. Lord, fix all my damaged places and make me whole once again. Use me for a special purpose in your Kingdom. Give me strength to endure the process that I must go through in order to be what you want me to be. I trust your will in my life. I place my life in your hands. In Jesus name, amen.

MY SCRIPTURES

2 Timothy 2:2, 2 Corinthians 4:7
Romans 8:18

As you read these scriptures daily, imagine yourself as being clay in the Father's hands. Remember that this is only a process, and none of your pain will be useless.

MY CHALLENGE: WEEK 3

Whether you realize it or not, we were all created for a specific purpose. That purpose will ultimately bring joy to Father God and help someone else. This week take a long look at your life. Take note of all the things that bring you inner happiness. This is connected to your divine purpose.

Find ways that you can use this talent, gift, or desire to change the life of someone else. You may love painting. Then paint something and give it away. You may love singing. Go sing to a group of people in a nursing home or hospital. Whatever you do that you enjoy more than anything, someone else will enjoy it too!

Remember, just like the clay on the potter's wheel - you are a work in progress. You don't have to be the best at what you do for God to get the glory out of it. All you need is a willing heart and availability to get it done.

The enemy will try to make you think you're looking like a fool because you have no(or very little) experience. Allowing others to see your flaws along the way will not make you look foolish, it will encourage them to find their purpose and share it as well. Remember, you are wonderfully flawed and you are a masterpiece in the hands of the Potter. Be a useful vessel in His hands.

MY PERSONAL JOURNAL

WEEK 3

MY GOALS:

MY ACCOMPLISHMENTS:

4 ~ MY BEAUTIFUL MESS

"Turn to me and be gracious to me, for I am lonely and afflicted. Relieve the troubles of my heart and free me from my anguish. Look on my affliction and my distress and take away all my sins." (Psalms 25:16-18)

You don't often find the words "beautiful" and "mess" in the same sentence. This profound contradiction can be used to describe your life at some point. It's like looking at the Weather Channel's image of a hurricane. From the safety of your home looking onto the television, it looks really spectacular. All the swirls and colors going in circles look absolutely amazing. We are in awe of the beauty of nature. But when you are in the eye of that storm, there's a total different perspective. It's not so beautiful from that point of view.

These terrible storms can come upon you so quickly that if you are not prepared, you can't run and take cover. You can name these storms Sickness, Infidelity, Grief, Rejection, Depression, Addiction, Failure, etc. Did you know that God can take the storm that the Enemy used for your destruction and turn it around for your divine destiny? Genesis 50:20 says, *"You intended to harm me, but God intended it for good to accomplish what is now being done, the saving of many lives."*

Don't ever curse the storms that you must endure. We will all have our share of them to go through. Buckle down and stay in the presence of the Lord and I promise He will see you through. Let the winds blow if they must. When it's all over, everything and everyone that still remains was meant to be there. Everyone who left while you were going through was blown away for a reason, let them go. God has a plan and a purpose for it all.

It may be hard to hold on, but your reward will be great in the end. You may slip up and say something out of character because of the agony. You are still a child of God, ask for forgiveness of that sin and keep holding on. Your testimony in the end will bring someone else out of their storm. Your experience is designed to strengthen you and give you wisdom to be a lifeline for someone who may not be able to stand alone. Count it all joy and know that God has a beautiful ending to this story. This is just a beautiful mess that you are going through.

Whether it was unexpected, or it was a mess that you created, you must trust God to fix what is broken in your life. He knows that you will mess up some things along the way. This is why a close relationship with Him is so important. You can call on Him, knowing that He will bring you out safely. Trust Him. Run to Him. Call on Him. He is your Heavenly Father, and He will give you shelter in the storms of life.

MY PRAYER: WEEK 4

Heavenly Father, thank you for being my shelter in the storms of this life. I sometimes create my own storms, but Lord there are other times when it seems like everything goes wrong and I am not at fault. Keep me in your loving arms and comfort me when I have no place to hide. I stand on your word knowing that this is all for your glory. Thank you for my measure of faith to get me through. I may be weak, but according to 2 Corinthians 12:9 Your grace is sufficient for me, and your power is made perfect in my weakness. I thank you, I honor you, and I praise you for a successful outcome. Use my testimony to bless others. In Jesus' name, amen.

MY SCRIPTURES

1 Peter 5:7, 1 Peter 5:10, 2 Corinthians 4:17, Romans 8:18

When you are going through a stormy situation, read these simple scriptures. All storms are temporary, they shall pass!

MY CHALLENGE: WEEK 4

We can all recall a time when God was the only one who worked something out in our lives. There was no other explanation! Every day this week I want you to write down a specific circumstance that you know for a fact that it had to be the hand of God on your life. A time that no one BUT GOD delivered you out of a beautiful mess. After recalling those stories, share them with someone else.

This exercise will not only encourage them, it will increase your faith the next time you go through a storm. Remembering what Father God has already done will remind you that "If He did it then, He will do it again."

Remember: Rev. 12:11 says, *"And they overcame him by the blood of the Lamb, and by the word of their testimony..."*

MY PERSONAL JOURNAL

WEEK 4

MY GOALS:

MY ACCOMPLISHMENTS:

5 ~ CHANGE

"See, I am doing a new thing! Now it springs up; do you not perceive it? I am making a way in the desert and streams in the wasteland." (Isaiah 43:19)

One thing that will always be true - change is inevitable. Nothing stays the same. The time, seasons, people, weather, habits, moods, everything changes. And although change is something that cannot be controlled, people are uncomfortable with it. I read a quote by Mark Twain that says, "The only person that likes change is a wet baby." Oh, how true is this statement.

As a child of God, there will be many changes that take place over time that will keep you in His will. You'll find that as your relationship grows with Him, your desires will change. This is the Holy Spirit guiding you. Your heart only wants to please God. These are good changes. But as with anything, with the good comes the bad. Any time you are trying to do the right thing, the Enemy will rare up to try to distract you from healthy change.

Father God places expiration dates on things that need to be removed from your life. He may allow certain people to stick around for a period of time. Just remember this, when the time comes for Him to hit the release button on some things that you are attached to, you better let them go. Don't drop the anchor in a place where God says to move away from. He is doing this for your own good. His will is that you grow to be a strong, wise disciple of Christ. Letting go is not always easy, but if you trust Him you'll find that His way is always the best for you.

In some cases, you may not be asked to let go. Sometimes people will walk out of your life, turn their backs on you, or leave you standing with your heart in your hand. Don't go chasing after them. Go means go. Let them go and you just continue to trust God. He has your path already laid out and your destination is set before you. Some people who started out on your path may have to take the next exit, but that's ok. Your journey is different from theirs. Keep it moving and stay in your own lane.

Be open to the new things that God is about to do in your life. Just because you have been blessed for the moment doesn't mean that's where God wants you to stay. Your Christian walk is all about growth and expanding. You will always experience change. In order for you to prosper and flourish, you must be willing to let Him do something new in you and through you. Get ready, hold onto His hand and embrace change. There is a great big blessing waiting for you. Let go of all that dead weight and make room for what this change is about to release into your life.

MY PRAYER: WEEK 5

Dear Heavenly Father, thank you so much for holding the plan of my life in your powerful hands. Although I realize that change is inevitable, I am uncomfortable with letting go of certain things or certain people. In my questionable moments, I will put my trust in you. Lead me in the right direction when I fail to see the way. Remove things from me when I don't know how to let go. Give me the courage to accept the changes that are set before me. Father I thank you for loving me enough not to let me go astray. When I sense that the time for change has come in my life, please let me know what your good and perfect will is for me. Then Lord, grant me the confidence I need to move out of the old and into the new place that you have for me. In Jesus name, amen.

MY SCRIPTURES

Hebrews 11:8, 1 Corinthians 13:11
Psalms 51:10-12

MY CHALLENGE: WEEK 5

When you consider the effect of change, your first thought may be having to adjust or get used to something out of the ordinary. But change can also be exciting when it comes to relationships. It's something we all need to experience from time to time. Even a change in the way we seek God can be exciting.

This week we want to change things up a bit. They say in order to keep relationships fresh, you have to do new things sometimes. The same goes for your relationship with God. You don't want to get bored by having the same old routine day in and day out. This is why so many people stop praying or studying His word. It becomes a boring routine, not exciting anymore. Don't ever allow your relationship to go stale with Him.

This week I want you to find some beautiful worship music or a nice poem of adoration to share with the Father. Play the songs and read the poems to Him! Buy some flowers and smell them as you study the word. Spend some extra time in pure worship, letting Him know how much you love Him. Changing things up in worship and praise brings excitement to both you and the Father. Be creative and do some extra-special things just for Him sometimes. He loves "just because" moments!

MY PERSONAL JOURNAL

WEEK 5

MY GOALS:

MY ACCOMPLISHMENTS:

6 ~ CHOICES

"Run from anything that stimulates youthful lusts. Instead, pursue righteous living, faithfulness, love, and peace. Enjoy the companionship of those who call on the Lord with pure hearts." (2 Timothy 2:22)

There is not a day that goes by when you won't have to make some kind of choice. We were created that way and it starts from birth. When you're a baby, you make a choice to just lay there wet and hungry, or to cry. As a child, you learn to choose which toy to play with. In school, you make a choice to study and do homework or fail all your classes. You choose what you want to do for a living, where to live, what to eat, what to wear, and the list goes on forever.

As a Christian, have you ever wondered why some fellow Christians "profess" to have faith while others are living a visibly blessed life? Some experience miracles and have great testimonies, while others just sit on the pews week after week. I'll tell you the difference - CHOICES. Your choices make you.

Just because you are born again doesn't mean you won't ever be tempted to sin. Actually you'll probably be tempted way more than the sinner if you aren't choosing to stay prayed up! Whatever your sin was before you came to Christ will be used as a weapon against you by the Evil One. This is why it is vitally important for you to stay connected to God by studying His word, praying, worshipping, and communing with Him regularly - not just on Sunday.

No one will ever force you to pray or study the word. God won't even force you to do it. That's a choice that only you can make. Your spiritual life depends on them. When the storms of life come crashing down upon you, the choices you made in the past will determine whether you sink or swim.

You best believe, trouble will come knocking at your door when you least expect it. Old friends will invite you to take part in their "fun". Married people will offer to take you out on a "friendly" date when you and your spouse are not getting along too well.. You'll see someone drop a wallet full of money when your bills are due. You have to recognize the tactics of the Devil. He uses your weakest moments to make you fall. Don't let him make a fool out of you. You know right from wrong. Your conscience works through the Holy Spirit, and it will convict you every time you make a wrong choice.

If you are ever put in a situation where you need to make a hard choice, pray about it. Don't ever make a decision without consulting God. A bad choice made in five seconds can cause you a lifetime of regret.

MY PRAYER: WEEK 6

Heavenly Father, help me when I have choices to make. I don't ever want to jump ahead of you and take matters into my own hands, but I want you to be the head of my life in all matters. You are the Way, Truth, and Light of my life and without you I cannot make it. Lord, forgive me for all the decisions I made without consulting you. From this day forward, I commit myself to seeking you fully before making choices and assuming that my way is the right way. Lead me every day of my life, in the direction you'd have me to go. Help me to say "no" when you say "no" and "yes" when you say "yes". In Jesus' name, amen.

MY SCRIPTURES

Matthew 7:13-14, Proverbs 14:12, Philippians 4:8, Isaiah 30:21, Matthew 6:1

There are several scriptures pertaining to making choices. Search the word for others, but keep these in your heart as well.

MY CHALLENGE: WEEK 6

You'd be amazed at how many decisions you make each day. Some small and some are big, but they all can have alternate outcomes. This week I want you to pay more attention to how many decisions you actually make each day. Allow yourself to feel like an outsider looking in, and be aware of just how many times you could have asked God for direction.

What were some of the results of your bad decisions?
How did praying for God's direction affect the outcome of a situation?

Once you see how many times you just leave God out of your decision making, you will be more in tune with Him and what He wants you to do. Take time to ask, "Lord, what will You have me to do?" He would love to hear from you.

MY PERSONAL JOURNAL

WEEK 6

MY GOALS:

MY ACCOMPLISHMENTS:

7 ~ THE VOICE OF GOD

"My sheep listen to my voice; I know them, and they follow me." (John 10:27)

The voice is unique to each individual. And even though we all sound differently, a child knows his parent's voice and the parent knows that child's voice. I can remember being at an amusement park filled with people. One of my sons had strayed away from the rest of us. I didn't realize it until I heard his cry. Out of all those people, I could hear the sound of my child's voice crying, "Mama!" I couldn't see him, but when I yelled out, "Here I am!"...he came running to me.

That's how it is with Father God. He can hear your cry. No matter how many people may be crying out, He specifically hears you. That's how you should be with hearing His voice. You need to be so in tune with Him that when He speaks, you know without a doubt that it's Him.

There are so many ways that He uses to communicate with you. When you have a daily relationship with Him, you will feel His guidance. It may be an unexplainable instinct, words that you hear in a song, or someone may say something to you confirming what you felt He was trying to tell you.

An active prayer life will sharpen your senses to hearing His voice. Reading the word of God regularly will help you become familiar with His character, which will open your heart to His voice. As you become closer to Him, you will begin to experience what some call "the voice of peace". This usually happens whenever you are making decisions. Whenever you are contemplating something and don't feel peaceful about it, that's His voice speaking to you. It's a great idea to stop and pray for direction when you feel this uneasiness.

One very important thing to remember is that when you feel like God is speaking to you, be quiet. Let Him speak. Never ignore the inner feeling, the peace, or instincts. He speaks regularly if you are active in prayer. What a joy to know that the Creator will speak to you! It makes my heart leap when I think about it.

We all find comfort in hearing the love in our parent's voice, just imagine the peace in hearing Father God...and knowing that it's definitely Him. You are His child, and He wants you to be sensitive to His voice. Just as He spoke to Moses, David, Daniel, Noah, and more...He will speak to you. All you have to do is talk to Him often, read and study His word, and always remember to have quiet, undisturbed moments set aside so that you can easily tune into His frequency. Believe me, of all the voices you'll ever hear in your life, His is the most important.

MY PRAYER: WEEK 7

My Heavenly Father, thank you for speaking to me today through this word. My greatest desire is to walk closer to you so that I will always hear your voice. Open my heart wider, enlighten me in your word, and always keep me near so that I will continue to feel your presence. Remove any distractions that may hinder me from hearing you. Help me to say the words of Samuel, "Speak Lord. Your servant hears." I love you with all my being, and I give you all the praise, glory, and honor for the great and mighty things you are doing in my life. Speak to me Lord, in Jesus' precious name, amen.

MY SCRIPTURES

James 4:8a, 1 Samuel 3:10b, Romans 8:14, Psalms 37:23-24, Jeremiah 29:12-13

MY CHALLENGE: WEEK 7

By now you should be noticing a closer relationship with Father God if you've been praying more than once daily, worshipping, and doing your challenges. Isn't this an exciting journey?! Learning to recognize the voice of God isn't as hard as some may think. If you do your part, He will definitely do His. As a matter of fact, He will do His part regardless. It's all up to you to do what it takes to hear Him.

This week you will focus on the many different ways God is speaking to you. Tell Him good morning, talk to Him from your heart just like you would talk to someone you love who may be standing in front of you. Soon you will notice "the voice of peace" speaking to you.

Your challenge is to take note each time you feel Him saying something. When that feeling comes, stop and close your eyes. Just breathe and listen. Write down how you feel, what you feel Him saying, and notice your surroundings. What kind of atmosphere is it? You will soon learn how to set the mood for His presence whenever you want to have that one-on-one time with Him. Learning to do this will make your worship time so much more special. There is nothing like having the Holy Presence of God readily available to you. This is a very special week. Enjoy every single moment of it.

MY PERSONAL JOURNAL

WEEK 7

MY GOALS:

MY ACCOMPLISHMENTS:

8 ~ YOUR DIVINE PURPOSE

"But when God, who set me apart from my mother's womb and called me by His grace was pleased to reveal His Son to me so that I might preach Him among the Gentiles, my immediate response was not to consult any human being." (Galatians 1:15-16 ESV)

There is a truth that you must always remember: God has a divine will and purpose for your life. That purpose will not only bring glory to Him, but it will bring you much joy as well. It doesn't end there. Your divine purpose will also mold you into living a life similar to Jesus. Hard to believe, but it's so true. If you are living your life and directing your purpose towards the will of God, you will naturally lead souls to the kingdom of God, just as Jesus did. This is the reason God placed purpose in your life. It's not to gain personal wealth, to become famous, or to be lifted up by others. It's to please the Father.

What is your purpose? It's connected to your gifts and talents. What do you love to do? What can you do that requires little or no effort at all? What do you do that makes you happy in your inner being? BINGO! This is where your purpose is attached. Your job is to find how you can use that "special thing" to bring glory to God. There is a way that you can use "it" to help others. Your job is to figure that part out.

In Acts 223:3 and Galatians 1:14, we see that Paul was a very intelligent, successful man. He held a high position in the community, and loved what he did. However, God had to blind him and knock him to the ground to get his attention. Seeking God for His will and direction is so much easier on you than having Him bring hardships upon you to get you on the right track.

The best way to find God's purpose for you is to quiet yourself (Psalms 46:10) and listen to God's still, small voice (1 Kings 19:12). Then you must willingly submit to His plans. Ask Him to reveal the plans and directions that were divinely laid out before you were born. He will gladly do it. He wants you to put His plan in action! Finding your purpose, and relying on God to accomplish it in a manner that is pleasing and acceptable to Him (Romans 12:1-2) is true success!

Remember these tips when trying to find your purpose: Try using your gifts in different ways to please God. Be patient and wait on God for revelation, you don't need a "back-up plan". Don't get caught up in "get rich quick schemes", they are not of God. Don't let people talk you into doing what they think you are called to do, learn to say "no" to man and "yes" to God. Finally, don't ever give up. The enemy will try to convince you that you will never be successful at what God has called you to do. Believe the voice of God! You are predestined for greatness.

MY PRAYER: WEEK 8

Heavenly Father, I thank you for giving my life purpose even before I was born. Today I declare that it's not my will, but your will be done in my life. I realize that my purpose is meant to bring glory to you.

Right now my life receives the anointing to prosper both spiritually and physically.

Right now my body receives divine healing and I am made whole so that I can effectively perform the duties associated to my purpose.

Right now my life and my destiny hear the word of the Lord and come out of the shadow of death and is alive in me.

Right now my calling begins to excel and propel with greatness.

Right now the works of my hands will prosper and bring forth glory to You.

Father God, arise in your glory and beautify my life. Allow divine connections for the benefit of my purpose and spiritual growth. Stir up the spirit of my divine partners and allow them to come looking for me. Destroy the agenda of the enemy that may delay or attempt to destroy my divine purpose. Let your eye of mercy see the situation of my life and cause it to change for your glory. In Jesus' precious and powerful name I pray, amen.

MY SCRIPTURES

Ecclesiastes 3:1-15, 2 Chronicles 28:8-11,
Isaiah 14:24-28, Exodus 9:16

MY CHALLENGE: WEEK 8

You may or may not know your purpose in life. Jeremiah 29:11 is a very popular scripture that lets us know that God has a plan for each one of us. This week, seek God in prayer and see if you can determine exactly what your purpose is. If you already know, then use this week seeking Him on new direction and ways to improve or expand what you are already doing. God always encourages growth, so don't get stagnant in your work. We all have room for expanding.

When God increases you in any way, you are to enlarge Him in every way. He's giving you new territory to allow you to claim new territory for the Kingdom! Remember, your purpose is about Him, not you. Your reward is great when you stick to the Father's plan, stay in His will, and work with a cheerful heart.

MY PERSONAL JOURNAL
WEEK 8

MY GOALS:

MY ACCOMPLISHMENTS:

9 ~ HE KEEPS HIS PROMISES

"You have kept your promises because you are righteous." (Nehemiah 9:8) "The Lord is faithful to all His promises and loving toward all He has made." (Psalms 145:13)

Have you ever been the victim of a broken promise? Someone assures you that they will do something and you put all your trust in their word, only to be let down. There was a time when peoples' word was as good as money, but today the promise or word of people is worthless. There are some people who are so good at breaking promises, we know not to trust anything they say.

On the other hand, have you made a promise to someone and something came up to prevent you from keeping your word? Don't you feel bad? A broken promise leads to a broken heart. There are times that we all fall short in even keeping promises we made to Father God. We should be thankful for His grace, mercy, and forgiveness.

While you may not always be able to put your trust in people, you can be assured that God keeps every promise. 2 Peter 3:9 reinforces our confidence in our faithful Father with these words, *"The Lord is not slack concerning His promise, as some men count slackness; but is longsuffering towards us, not willing that any should perish, but that all should come to repentance."*

He keeps His promises to you because He wants to meet all your needs. He wants you to trust Him completely in every area of your life. Once you totally surrender your life to Him, you will understand what this means. Your relationship with Him is so important to the success and happiness of your life.

This leads to a very critical part of receiving those promises- obedience. Yes, I said obedience. Would you give your child a reward if she/he was disobedient to you? Our Father requires the same thing from us. Living according to His will and His word is the key to receiving His promises. You won't always get it right. There will be times when you fail, you stumble, you get lazy, etc. Just remember that we serve a Father who is always leading you in the right direction. Ask Him to forgive you for the times you rebel against what you know is right. He is patient and loving enough to stay right there, even in your stubbornness.

God never gives up on you, and you should never give up on Him. He will keep every promise. It may not come in your time, but when you trust Him with your whole heart you will see them come to pass. Sure, it may seem like He's forgotten you but He hasn't. You're a priority in His eyes, and He will never forsake you. You can count on that! Believe it!!

MY PRAYER: WEEK 9

Dear Heavenly Father, I thank you today for every promise you've made to me. I am so grateful that you keep every one of them. Sometimes I wonder if I am even worthy of all of these promises, but I know that I am through Jesus Christ. Lord, forgive me for the times I didn't make decisions according to your will. Clean my heart so that I may walk upright before you. I want to live pleasing in your sight. I want to be an obedient child and receive all the best you have promised me. I love you and I thank you for loving me. I claim every promise in Jesus name, amen.

MY SCRIPTURES

Hebrews 10:23, 2 Peter 1:1-4, 2 Peter 3:9,
Isaiah 25:1, Philippians 4:7

MY CHALLENGE: WEEK 9

There are literally hundreds of promises from the Lord in the Bible, so needless to say we won't go over all of them here. I do want to enlighten you about a few of them this week. Read these scriptures that apply to each promise and allow them to penetrate your heart. Your challenge is to write down some of the promises of God that have been visible in your life. This will help you to see just how much God is doing in your life, things that you may have taken for granted. Give Him praise for each one!

Wisdom for every challenge you may face: James 1:5
Peace in times of trouble: Philippians 4:6-7
The desires of your heart: Psalms 37:4
Guidance and instruction: Psalms 32:8
Guarantee of God's love: Romans 8:38-39
Provision for your daily needs: Matthew 6:25-32
His presence wherever you go: Deuteronomy 31:8
Strength in difficult times: Isaiah 41:10
Forgiveness of your sins: 1 John 1:9
Answer to your prayers: 1 John 5:14-15
Healing for wounds and diseases: Psalms 103:1-3

God loves you so much, and has promised all these things plus hundreds more! Studying His word regularly will reveal all the wonderful promises to you. I encourage you to stay before Him in prayer and worship so that you will stay in His will and qualify to receive them. Oh how He loves me and you! Doesn't it feel good to know just how much He cares?

MY PERSONAL JOURNAL

WEEK 9

MY GOALS:

MY ACCOMPLISHMENTS:

10 ~ WAKE UP YOUR DEAD DREAMS

"Now to him that is able to do exceeding abundantly above all that we ask or think, according to the power that works in us." (Ephesians 3:20)

One of my favorite mottos is "Dreams are God's way of allowing us to see through His eyes." I say that to myself quite often, especially when I get discouraged about something that I know I should be doing but it seems impossible. This opening passage of scripture instills the fact that there is nothing impossible with God.

Dreams are what God uses to increase our faith. We know that without Him, we could not accomplish them. Throughout your lifetime, you will have more than one dream. God gives them to you to create your destiny. Your destiny is actually the sum of all your dreams!

No matter who you are, there will be many obstacles in your way as you pursue the desires of your heart. Be prepared to roll up your sleeves because you are in for a fight. God promised to be with you, but He never said it was going to be an easy journey. One of the keys to success is "never give up." If you choose to quit in order to take the easy way out or to skip all the pain and challenges, I have news for you: a life of misery awaits. If you aren't doing what you know deep in your heart you should be doing, you will never be completely happy. There will always be a void in your life.

Wake up your dead dreams, they don't have to die. Be aware that things happen and sometimes circumstances will cause you to get off track. You make a wrong turn and suddenly feel lost or overwhelmed. That's OK, just don't give up. You will run into road blocks along the way. There will be failures, grief, tragedy, disappointment, and rejection somewhere along the journey to success. The most important thing for you to know today is that no matter what your journey takes you to, He is faithful to see you through it. *"He has engraved your face upon the palm of His hand and He does not forget."* (Isaiah 49:16).

As a child of God, your future journey has a promise, but you may not always see the roadmap. Go forth by faith, knowing that He has a plan and it will all work out for your good. There are people out there waiting to be blessed by the dream God placed within you. Sure, you will be blessed too! Just know that it's about the kingdom first. (Read Matthew 6:33).

As you travel the road to your destiny, be sure to take your time. Enjoy the little blessings along the way. Smell the flowers, enjoy the sunshine, listen to the birds singing in the morning. The destination will be wondrous, but the scenery along the way will always live on in your heart, knowing that Father God was with you all the way.

MY PRAYER: WEEK 10

Father God, thank you for placing the dreams inside my heart. You know why they were given to me, and I trust that you will guide me along the troublesome roads to accomplish them. My spirit leaps for joy knowing that you didn't create me to be normal. Thank you for the example of Jesus Christ, living a life of risk-taking. Order my steps in your word so that I may not get overwhelmed along the way. Give me strength when I am weak, encouragement when I am low, and courage when I am afraid. Your word says in Psalms 35:7 that you will help me if I commit my work unto you. Today I commit all my work unto you, Father. Establish my dreams that they may bring glory to You and be a blessing to others. In Jesus' name, amen.

MY SCRIPTURES

1 Thessalonians 5:16-18, Proverbs 13:12, Jeremiah 29:11

MY CHALLENGE: WEEK 10

As children of God, we should all have a dream instilled within our hearts. There is something deep inside that's just burning to come out of you. You weren't created to be empty inside. That inner dream is much larger than your outer being, that's why it's tearing you apart, trying to get out.

This week you will identify that dream, if you haven't already. Take it to God in sincere prayer and ask Him to bring it to life! You may have to take it to Him more than once. I want you to feel it come alive deep inside your soul. Talk about it, think about it, concentrate on it, and start making it a part of you.

Your challenge is to take at least one step each day towards making that dream come into existence. Make the phone calls. Pray for divine connections. Research the business, sign up for classes, find a mentor in that field and follow their guidelines. The focus is DO SOMETHING! When you don't know what to do, pray. You have to feel this thing jumping out of your body. God didn't put a dream inside for you to let it dry up and die.

Remember: when someone gives you a gift, they like to see you use and enjoy it! Show God what you can do with that dream and He'll show you how great He can work through it.

MY PERSONAL JOURNAL

WEEK 10

MY GOALS:

MY ACCOMPLISHMENTS:

11 ~ ACCOUNTABILITY

"Whoever conceals his transgressions will not prosper, but he who confesses and forsakes them will obtain mercy." (Proverbs 28:13)

The word "accountability" makes a lot of people uncomfortable. They want to talk about all the blessings of God but never want to touch on the subjects that chastise us or makes us walk the straight and narrow.

There are two sides of accountability. One is being held accountable, or accepting the blame for our wrong-doing. This is the act of going before God in prayer to confess our sins to Him and repent. But this week I want to focus on another act of accountability.

As Christians, it is imperative that you find an accountability partner or a few partners whom you trust and love to encourage, inspire, and motivate you to stay in the will of God, and you can do the same for them. Your accountability partner is someone you can be vulnerable and totally honest with and trust enough that they won't gossip about your personal issues. Their purpose is to promote spiritual growth. They aren't afraid to tell you the raw truth, they stand between you and a poor choice. God will place someone in your life just for that purpose if you ask Him.

Accountability means you will be able to confess your weaknesses, share burdens, testify of God's goodness, uplift, correct, and help fight the battles of life. James 5:16 tell us that we should confess our sins to each other so that we may be healed. In Ephesians chapter 4 we learn about unity in the body of Christ. Paul tells us about the importance of Christians encouraging and holding each other up. You can't live a Christian life alone. Without encouragement and support from other

Christians you'll become weak. Satan wants to weaken your relationship with other Christians so that he can destroy your relationship with Father God.

Who should be your accountability partner? Obviously, they should be Christian. Attach yourself to someone stronger in faith than you, so that you can become stronger. Be sure not to partner with someone who has the same weaknesses as you. If you were an alcoholic, you don't need to be connected with another former alcoholic. You may both get weak at the same time, and no one will overcome! Be sure they are the same sex as you. Sharing personal information with the opposite sex can open doors for the enemy to attack you both. They should have an active prayer life. Basically, they should be who you want to become in Christ. The best accountability partner would be whoever God places in your life to fill that role. He already has someone to fill that position especially for you.

MY PRAYER: WEEK 11

Dear Heavenly Father, I just want to thank you for loving me enough to never leave me alone. Thank you for showing your love for me in every way. Lord, my desire is to grow stronger in faith. I know that you have assigned people ordained especially to walk with me on this Christian journey. Bring that person or people predestined to walk with me, into my life now. Give me a desire to live a righteous life. Help me to not only be accountable to someone else, but to also be a great partner for someone else to be accountable to. I pray to you in Jesus' holy name, amen.

MY SCRIPTURES

James 5:16, Ephesians Chapter 4, Job 31:33,
2 Samuel 12:13, 1 Corinthians 12:27, 2 Corinthians 13:11,
1 Timothy 3:7

MY CHALLENGE: WEEK 11

Accountability is something that most success coaches teach their clients. They say if you share your goals with someone else, it gives you motivation to work towards reaching those goals. The same applies to Christian accountability partners. If you have someone to confess your weaknesses, trials, accomplishments, and goals to then you will become more motivated to live in the will of God.

This week you will pray and seek out to find one or two accountability partners. I don't encourage you to look for more than two. Sit down and explain to them what an accountability partner is and why you feel they should be yours.

Once this person agrees to be your partner, start your journey with them by praying together. Share testimonies about things God has done to change your lives. Share dreams, goals, struggles, and weaknesses. You are building a new type of relationship, so take care of it. Keep all conversations strictly between you. Vow to have each other's back when the enemy attacks. Most of all encourage each other by studying the word of God and applying it to your lives. Be honest with each other, agree to be the wedge between them and a wrong choice. Remember, temptation loses its grip in the face of accountability.

MY PERSONAL JOURNAL

WEEK 11

MY GOALS:

MY ACCOMPLISHMENTS:

12 ~ MY WEAKNESS, HIS STRENGTH

Three times I pleaded with the Lord to take it away from me. But He said to me, "My grace is sufficient for you, for my power is made perfect in weakness." Therefore I will boast all the more gladly about my weaknesses, so that Christ's power may rest on me. That is why, for Christ's sake I delight in weaknesses, in insults, in hardships, in persecutions, in difficulties. For when I am weak, then I am strong. (2 Corinthians 12:8-10)

If there ever was a scripture to help you get through hard times, this would be the one. No matter who you are, there will come a day when you cannot make it on your own. You'll need the power of Jesus Christ to bring you through a helpless situation.

It's easy to praise God when things are going good. But when that storm of life comes beating at your door and all hell breaks loose, all you can do is fall on your knees and surrender. You may even find yourself praying for God to work a miracle to get you out of the situation as quickly as possible. When God doesn't come to your aid as fast as you want Him to, it's easy to get frustrated and lose hope. Paul said in this text that he asked God three times to take it away from him, but He did not come.

One thing you must know is that God hears your cry, and He will answer. He will allow you to go through the hardships long enough for you to realize that you are not in control. He will get the glory out of this. You've got to relinquish all control, and let Him take charge in order to come out victorious. God doesn't need your help, he just desires your obedience and faith in Him.

The biggest obstacle that will cause a delay in your rescue is pride. You think you can fix it. You have been self-sufficient and solved so many problems on your own. You know it was God who blessed you to come this far, but now you're taking control of everything. Until you understand that all you have belongs to Him, your pride will set you up for destruction. 2 Chronicles 26:16 tells us that *"His pride led to his downfall."*

Although not all hardships come from pride, you must be aware that pride is involved with how quickly you release it all to God. No matter what the problem may be, remember what Psalms 18:32 says, *"It is God who gives me strength and makes my way perfect."*

No matter how weak you get, if you put your trust in Him, he promised to never leave you alone. Learn to activate your faith. Believe the word of God and know that strength is found in Him when you are weak. Let go of self-sufficiency and lay your cares before Him, and leave them there. I promise you that He will show himself mighty and strong. There is nothing too hard for God. He loves you and gives you strength to endure. This is only a storm, and it shall pass.

MY PRAYER: WEEK 12

Father God, I come to you today thanking you for being my strength when I am weak. I am so grateful for you being there to sustain me when I don't know whether I'm coming or going. Lord help me to put all my trust in you. Sometimes things get so hard and I get frustrated, upset, and even nervous about what to do next. I realize that in these situations, I am helpless. I'm calling on you, Lord. I give it all to you. Help me in this time of need. Only you can fix it. I can do nothing without you. Thank you for taking this burden from me. All glory belongs to you. You've done marvelous things and you continue to work all things out for my good. For this I praise you. I walk in victory because of you. Strengthen me and bless me to endure until you come. In Jesus' name, amen.

MY SCRIPTURES

Psalms 18, Isaiah 40:29, Isaiah 40:31,
Psalms 34:8, Exodus 15:2

MY CHALLENGE: WEEK 12

We all have strengths and weaknesses. You may have a strong prayer life, but you don't really study the word like you should. That's just a simple example, but strengths and weaknesses run much deeper than this. Your strengths can sometimes cause pride to set in. You may be good at making money, and then you soon forget that it's God who gives you that knowledge. You may the best athlete, actor, chef, teacher, carpenter, story-teller, garbage man, plumber, or mechanic. Just know that without God, you wouldn't be anything. Your weaknesses can also be a downfall. You may have a weakness to alcohol, drugs, sex, theft, cigarettes, or lying. Even though God delivered you from that sin, there still may be something that triggers that desire.

This week you will acknowledge (write down) your strengths. One by one I want you to recognize how God is the reason you're so strong in these areas. Take some special time to thank Him for these strengths and figure out a way to use them for His glory. Likewise, write down your weaknesses. Realize that without the hand of God on your life, these weaknesses could overtake you at any given moment. Ask God to give you divine strength to be able to resist temptation in these areas. Pray for His protection and thank Him for victory over them. When you give glory to God for every strength and weakness, you will build faith and find it easier to surrender to His will when the storms of life come upon you. He will deliver!

MY PERSONAL JOURNAL

WEEK 12

MY GOALS:

MY ACCOMPLISHMENTS:

13 ~ THE COMPANY YOU KEEP

"Do not be misled: Bad company corrupts good character." (1 Corinthians 15:33)

You've probably heard the old saying, "One bad apple spoils the whole bunch." This is such a true statement. It doesn't just apply to the fruit! No matter who you are, the enemy has some "bad apples" out there waiting to try to corrupt you.

They can come in the form of old friends who used to do things with you...things you have now been delivered from. When you decide to walk with Christ, you must be very careful about the company you keep. Don't let yourself think that you are strong enough to fight any battle alone. The enemy will trick you into thinking you won't be affected by the wrong company. His purpose is to get you alone, so he can go in for the kill.

You may think all the bible scriptures you've learned and all the bible classes you've attended will be enough to withstand, but I'm here to tell you that just is not so. If you read about Solomon, you'll see that God granted him great wisdom but that did not keep him from turning to other gods. Why did Solomon do that? It was because of the wives he married. They were a source of bad company. They corrupted his morals and turned his heart away. (1 Kings 11:4)

As a child of God it is very important for you to surround yourself with other Christians. Get together with them often and enjoy their company. The enemy wants you to think you're missing out on something. My friend, the only thing you're missing out on is a burning hell! You are only as strong as the weakest person in your circle of friends. If you are the strongest one in your circle then it's time to become part of another circle. Not saying you must break friendship with your current group, but you need to move on and surround yourself with constant growth. Find stronger Christians to associate with, and do what they do to grow! It's through your spiritual growth that you will be equipped to witness to those "bad apples".

Be cautious of the people who you allow to keep your attention. The enemy uses sweet words, jokes, entertainment, and things that feel good as tools to weaken your spirit. Before you know it you're skipping prayer time. Then you don't have time to read the word. Then suddenly you're wondering what happened and how did it happen so fast! Look at your friends as shields of protection for your spiritual life. If they aren't helping you stay safe from the enemy, then they aren't good for you. Take your spiritual life seriously. Jesus didn't die on that cross for your salvation for you to walk in the company of wolves. Protect what God gave you by any means necessary.

MY PRAYER: WEEK 13

Dear Heavenly Father, thank you for loving me enough to save my soul. My desire is to grow closer to you every day. Help me to be careful of the company I keep. My salvation is precious and I don't take it for granted. Give me friends who will enhance my spiritual growth and encourage me to stay in your will. Help me to be a good friend to other Christians. In Jesus' name, amen.

MY SCRIPTURES

1 Peter 5:8, 1 Corinthians 15:58, 1 Corinthians 6:9, Proverbs 13:20

MY CHALLENGE: WEEK 13

The company you keep is a reflection of you. You are a product of your environment. This is why as a child of God, you must be mindful of your close friendships.

This week I want you to do a little evaluation of your inner circle. Your relationship with God is too important for you to allow toxic relationships to affect your spiritual life. If you need to make adjustments in who you are around, now is the time to do that. Get closer to the people who strengthen you, and distance yourself from the ones that may come between you and the Father.

Cleaning up your life doesn't mean you have to throw away people you've known for years and developed friendships with. Just use this lesson to witness to them. If you love them, you'll want to see them in the family of God along with you. Team up with some of your Christian friends and ask God to make a way for you to witness to them. This is a great opportunity for you to get comfortable sharing Jesus!

You don't have to shove the bible down their throat. Just let the Spirit lead you. Sometimes just being a shoulder to cry on, or a soft heart to help comfort a broken heart will be the open door. Your goal is to clean up your surroundings. No better way to start than with the people who knew you while you were in your mess. You are the ideal person to witness to them. And don't forget, be prayerful and don't allow them to drag you down. You are pulling them up! Let's take care and be watchful of the company we keep.

MY PERSONAL JOURNAL

WEEK: 13

MY GOALS:

MY ACCOMPLISHMENTS:

14 ~ NEVER ALONE

"At my first defense, no one came to my support, but everyone deserted me. May it not be held against them. But the Lord stood at my side and gave me strength, so that through me the message might be fully proclaimed and all the Gentiles might hear it. And I was delivered from the lion's mouth. The Lord will rescue me from every evil attack and will bring me safely to His heavenly kingdom. To Him be glory forever and ever. Amen." (2 Timothy 4:16-18)

Loneliness has become an epidemic in this big world in which we live. It's hard to believe that many countries are over populated, yet so many people are suffering from loneliness. We were created to be relational, and when we are separated from people it can be very discouraging. Unfortunately, it even happens in the Christian community.

You can be in a stadium filled with people or in a room all by yourself and still feel the effects of loneliness. It can come from the loss of a loved one, rejection, broken friendships, relocation, new school, or many other reasons. The fact is, loneliness is unmistakably a major problem in many lives. But it doesn't have to be that way, especially if you're a child of God.

The Enemy loves to pour salt into your wounds, making you think that no one cares about you and you're not loved or appreciated. Don't you dare listen to those lies. You can be alone, but not lonely. God promised you in Hebrews 13:5 that He would never leave or forsake you. I'm here to tell you today that there is no place in Heaven or on Earth that is unreachable to God. Rest assured in knowing that whatever you are going through, He is right there with you - whether you feel Him or not! It's during these lonely times when you may not feel His presence, but you must hold on to the true fact that He is there. His word is true.

Did you know that God has a purpose for these lonely times? So many times I've experienced that during my lonely moments is when I can hear from Him more clearly. Use this time to talk to Father God. Study and meditate on His word so that you can get into His presence. After all, if you're alone this is the best time to talk to Him. Pour your heart out, let the tears flow. Let Him comfort you. His love for you is so deep and so powerful that nothing can come between you and Him. Trust and believe that when you need a Comforter, He is only a breath away.

You may be lonely, but dear friend, you are never alone. Find peace in His presence. There is nothing that can fill a void like the presence of your Creator. He loves you and cares for you like no one else can. Jesus died for you! That's just how much He cares. This loneliness is temporary. It will pass. Praise God now for bringing you out of it stronger and even more beautiful for His glory.

MY PRAYER: WEEK 14

Heavenly Father, thank you for never leaving me alone. Even during my loneliest days, I can find comfort in knowing that you are here with me. Whenever I get too weak to pray, help me to still find peace in knowing that you are with me and you understand all my sorrows. Fill every empty place in my heart with your presence. In Jesus' name, amen.

MY SCRIPTURES

2 Corinthians 9:8, Hebrews 13:5, Joshua 1:9
Isaiah 43:1-3, Isaiah 43:13, Ephesians 3:14-16, Matthew 28:20

MY CHALLENGE: WEEK 14

Take advantage of your loneliness. Make it work for your good. There is strength in the word of God and in His presence. If you are going through the valley of loneliness, spend some quality time in the word of God. Read the following stories and take note of the characteristics of God in each one. How does it relate to you? Put yourself in the stories and allow God to do the same for you.

Psalms Chapter 71, David's story.
2 Timothy 4:6-22, Paul's story.
1 Kings 19:1-18, Elijah's story.

Sometimes when we are lonely, we fall into the Enemy's trap of becoming focused on ourselves. This selfish "poor me" attitude can cause you to slip into a deep depression. If you are lonely, then you need to get busy for the Lord. Visit a nursing home, hospital, or help with a homeless shelter. Giving out of your emptiness is the perfect set-up for God to bring joy into your heart.

You may be weak and lonely now, but don't plan on staying that way. God created you to be a light for others. Are you going to have struggles? Certainly. Will you always have the zeal to bless others? Of course not. But now is the time for you to shake yourself and stand up in the enemy's face. Let him know that even though you may be in a little rut right now, you are coming out victorious!

The joy of the Lord is your strength. Your heart may be lonely, but your hands are blessed. Put them to work. Your feet are blessed, go out and tell somebody about His goodness. If you are still breathing, you need to use that breath to give God some praise! Reach beyond yourself.

MY PERSONAL JOURNAL

WEEK 14

MY GOALS:

MY ACCOMPLISHMENTS:

15 ~ SELF IMAGE

"I praise you because I am fearfully and wonderfully made; your works are wonderful, I know that full well." (Psalms 139:14)

When you look in your mirror, do you like what you see? These are the days of plastic surgery, Botox, implants, and everything false. No one seems to like what they see. Society dictates whether you are too fat or too thin, too tall or too short, and too dark or too light. How do you see yourself?

We all have flaws, but if you see yourself less than remarkable or only ordinary then you aren't seeing yourself as God sees you. Father God created you to be magnificent. You are His divine creation, His masterpiece. Just the thought of being made in His image should be overwhelming.

The scripture for this week tells you how fearfully and wonderfully made you are. Have you ever considered that it goes far beyond the natural image? Your soul bears the image of God. This is why we have a mind, will, and emotions. And if you read Ephesians 4:24 and Colossians 3:10 you'll learn that God's image also consists of knowledge, righteousness, and true holiness.

Human beings were not created like other creatures. We have the ability to make moral judgments and we can discern right from wrong. We have pride, shame, and guilt to direct our decisions. We can recognize wrong and expect to have redemption.

God also created us to be in relationship with Him. He wants us to willfully seek Him and live a prosperous life. He doesn't want us to see Him as a big monster in the sky. He gets joy when we love and adore Him. We are family. Once we realize the true image in which we were created, only then will we truly be happy with who we are.

This body will pass away. It doesn't matter if it's fat, skinny, tall, short, black, or white. It has to go back to the dust from which it was formed. But that beautiful creation inside will live on to be with Father God. You are an eternal creation. You are the very image of God himself. Take pride in who you are. Walk in authority.

There is no reason for you to ever look down on yourself. God created you just the way you are. If anyone has a problem with that, let them take it up with the Maker. Your job is to live a life that is pleasing to Him. Your outer appearance has absolutely nothing to do with beauty. You are the image of God. That alone should give you confidence in yourself. He is the Master of creating masterpieces. Give Him praise for the work He put in especially for you. There is no one else like you, God intended it to be that way!

MY PRAYER: WEEK 15

Father God, thank you for making me in your image. Forgive me for ever thinking that I am less than good enough. Forgive me for believing lies that others have told me concerning my appearance. The fact that you love me and accept me is far more important to me than what others may think when they look at me. I am so honored that you would care enough to create me in your image. I am amazing. I am wonderfully made. I am your child and that's good enough. Help me to walk in righteousness and true holiness. I want to be even more like you. In Jesus' name, amen.

MY SCRIPTURES

Genesis 1:26-27, Matthew 10:30, Job 38:36, Luke 12:7

MY CHALLENGE: WEEK 15

Self image is something that many people tend to struggle with these days. If we take the word "self" out of that problem, then we can focus on just "image".

Do you ever wonder what people think about you when you walk away? As a child of God, you should care about this because you are representing Father God. The image you project to others should reflect love, hope, victory, and joy.

This week I want you to take a real good look at your image. Not your physical image in the mirror, but your spiritual image. Are you reflecting your heavenly Father? What can you do to be more like Him?

Take time out each day to think before you act. Be a little more patient. Show a little more love to those who you tend to avoid. Put on the mind of Christ when dealing with others. This week is all about changing your image. You should "look like" a child of God in everything you do.

MY PERSONAL JOURNAL

WEEK 15

MY GOALS:

MY ACCOMPLISHMENTS:

16 ~ FAITH REVEALED

"He replied, "Because you have so little faith. I tell you the truth, if you have faith as small as a mustard seed, you can say to this mountain, 'move from here to there' and it will move. Nothing will be impossible for you." (Matthew 17:20)

When you say the word "faith" what comes to mind? I know it seems like a simple question, but most Christians have a passive attitude when you discuss faith. Even though you only need a little faith to move the hand of God, it is very important for you to understand the true elements of faith.

Many people have been taught that faith is blind. That is totally not true. God would never have you blinded. The word of God is to enlighten you. You will not be blinded by His word. Faith is placing your confidence in someone or something because that person or thing has proven to be trustworthy! Let's look at the three elements of faith.

The first element is "knowledge". It is based on certain fundamental truths. Knowing that God is Creator. Knowing that Jesus is the Son of God. Knowing that He will do what He says He will do. When you know something, that alone is power. Knowledge is power...(Proverbs 24:5).

The second element is "belief". It is not enough to just know something, you must believe that it is true. This element is written all through the book of John. (5:46-47, 8:31-38, 10:37-38, 14:11). When you know and believe in something, there is no way anyone can convince you otherwise.

The third element is "trust". Without this element, the other two are useless. Trusting in God shows that you have put all your confidence in Him. You won't be easily swayed from your belief. Psalms 37:5 says, *"Commit your way to the Lord; trust in*

Him, and He will act." Trust is built on knowledge and belief. If you have the love of God in you, then you must trust in Him.

When you combine all three of these elements, you will have perfect faith. Not only the mustard seed faith, but great faith! When true faith exists, there is nothing that will limit the power of God in your life. This true faith will cause manifestation to take place in all the seemingly impossible circumstances that come your way.

Today God is calling you to step out in true faith, not blind faith. Matthew 19:26 reminds you that *"with man this is impossible, but with God all things are possible."* Activate your faith today by building your knowledge, belief, and trust in Him. This is the only way to grow your faith. Remember that it is during times of uncertainty that we strengthen our faith in God. Growing and strengthening our faith pleases Him. Without faith it is impossible to please God. (Hebrews 11:6)

MY PRAYER: WEEK 16

Heavenly Father, I am so grateful for learning about how to strengthen my faith. It is my heart's desire to please you. I know that in order to do that, I must have faith. Today Lord, I commit all my thinking to your will and your word. Forgive me when my faith has been weak. Open my heart to receive more and more of you so that my faith will be true. Help me to lean on your understanding and not my own. I praise and honor you for all you've done and all that I'm believing you to do. From this day forth, I walk in true faith. In Jesus' name, amen.

MY SCRIPTURES

Hebrews Chapter 11, 2 Corinthians 5:7, Psalms 119:105
James 2:26, John 20:31, Psalms 71:5-6, Proverbs 3:5-6
Psalms 37:5

MY CHALLENGE: WEEK 16

There comes a time when your faith will be tested. The word says without faith it is impossible to please God. If your goal is to please Him, then you must do all you can to perfect the measure of faith He has given you.

This week I want you to honestly take a look at your "faith meter". Do you really know, believe, and trust God as much as you should? We have all come up short at some point in our lives. Take this week to study the scriptures in this week's devotion.

Your challenge for the week is to put your faith to work. There is something in your heart that only God can handle. Will you trust Him to take care of it? Can you let it go completely and allow God to do what only He can do in this situation? He would be so pleased if you did!

Sometimes we get caught up in a sea of troubles because we try to fix things ourselves. Now is the time to live above SEE LEVEL. Let go and let God. That is your assignment.

MY PERSONAL JOURNAL

WEEK 16

MY GOALS:

MY ACCOMPLISHMENTS:

Congratulations on completing your first 16 weeks of devotions! These past weeks were directed towards helping you to develop a sincere relationship with Father God through Jesus Christ and the Holy Spirit. In the next several chapters we will directly approach many struggles, roadblocks, and forms of spiritual bondage that must be confronted, confessed, and forgiven in order for you to live free and peaceful. We are laying it all on the altar so that deliverance can take place. Allow the Holy Spirit to lead you to the Throne of Grace as you get rid of the things that have held you captive. Get ready for your new life in Christ. The best is yet to come!

17 ~ PURSUIT OF PERFECTION

"And if you greet only your brothers, what are you doing more than others? Do not even pagans do that? Be perfect, therefore, as your heavenly Father is perfect." (Matthew 5:47-48 NIV)

"If all you do is love the lovable, do you expect a bonus? Anybody can do that. If you simply say hello to those who greet you, do you expect a medal? Any run-of-the-mill sinner does that. In a word, what I am saying is, grow up. You're kingdom subjects. Now act like it. Live out your God-created identity. Live generously and graciously toward others, the way God lives toward you. " (Matthew 5:46-48 The Message Bible)

The definition of perfection is: complete; wanting for nothing necessary. Jesus Christ was the only human who ever lived a perfect life. He was the very seed of God, so no sin ever lived in Him. As for us, we were born in sin, never to be perfect or spotless. So what did Jesus mean when He said, "Be perfect"? Is that humanly possible?

Since we were all born in sin, we must be washed in the blood of Jesus to cleanse us of it. Accepting Him as your Savior is only one step towards a perfect life. The word tells us in Mark 10:18 that "there is none perfect but the Father". When Jesus says "be perfect", He was giving us a goal. As a child of God, you should strive to live as close to the pattern Jesus set for us as possible.

When God created man in the beginning, we were intended to be perfect. Sin destroyed that. But Jesus came to give us hope for a perfect destiny. The key is to move towards and not away from perfection. You must turn away from your own thinking and desires and allow the Holy Spirit to direct you through the steps that God has already prepared for you. Nothing you ever do will be perfect, only God is perfect. But if you allow Him to work through you, then you will live a life that is pleasing to Him.

Perfection is a standard. Direction is your test. It's totally up to you to surrender to the will of God. Know that you can do all things through Christ which strengthens you. (Philippians 4:13) Change your way of thinking and the words you say. Stop speaking failure. Don't say, "Well, I'm only human." No you're not! If you have been saved, you are a conqueror through Christ Jesus! You are more than human and you have the power of God working in you to overcome anything that would cause you to fall.

Once you know who you are and whose you are, then perfection will be your goal. Will you mess up sometimes? Yes you will. But God is a forgiving and merciful God. He just wants to see you do your very best to walk in His way. If you focus on the goal and not the obstacles, He will be very proud of you.

MY PRAYER: WEEK 17

Heavenly Father, thank you for wanting the very best for me. Although I realize that no one is perfect but You, I am called to try my best to live as close to perfection as I can. I cannot do anything in my own power, but with You working in me, I can do so much better than I have in the past. Thank you for grace and mercy following me all the days of my life. Empower me to live the way you desire. Strengthen me when I am weak and guide me every day. Hold me when I slip and pick me up when I fall. In Jesus name I pray, amen.

MY SCRIPTURES

Romans 3:23, Romans 3:10, Colossians 3:12-14
James 1:19-20, Ephesians 4:32, Luke 6:31, Philippians 2:2-8,
Ephesians 2:10

MY CHALLENGE: WEEK 17

No one is perfect. Only God can fit that description. But now that we know His desire is for us to live as close to His way as we can, let's try our very best. Doesn't He deserve your best effort?

This week should be quite interesting. I'm not going to ask you to be squeaky clean. But I do want you to be more aware of your not-so-perfect habits, words, and thoughts.

Your challenge this week is to see if you can change the way you respond to the way you handle day to day situations. Pay attention and stop the hurtful or negative words from coming out of your mouth. When you want to gossip or degrade someone, find something nice to say about them instead. Give a helping hand to someone you'd normally ignore. Smile when you feel like blowing up.

There are so many things that can be changed or stopped if we would only allow the Holy Spirit to work and speak through us. You are a Kingdom citizen and you represent Father God. Let that show each day by the way you react, work, and speak. Enjoy this week. Pray for God to do a new thing in your efforts. Make Him proud to call you His son or daughter. Seek perfection in all you do, according to His power that lives in you.

MY PERSONAL JOURNAL

WEEK 17

MY GOALS:

MY ACCOMPLISHMENTS:

18 ~ FEAR OF REJECTION

"I sought the Lord, and He answered me; He delivered me from all my fears." (Psalms 34:4)

The pain of rejection can run deep and pierce your heart like a hot knife. We were created to desire love from others. Everyone wants to be loved and accepted and when we aren't, we feel humiliated. No one can tell how much rejection hurts you just by looking. 1 Corinthians 2:11 tells us that *"no one knows what anyone else is thinking or what he is really like except that person himself."*

Rejection will cause you to wear a happy face mask when you are in public, when all the while there are tears flowing inside. If you've ever been rejected, and felt that deep pain that comes along with it, you can easily become afraid to be rejected again. This is called the fear of disapproval. Proverbs 29:25 says, *"The fear of human opinion disables."* You fear that you aren't good enough. Maybe you don't fit in because of your financial status, race, weight, or education level. The fact is, people spend far too much time trying to impress or earn acceptance from others. They go out of the way and do so much to try to be loved and accepted. Many times these are things out of their character.

The affects of rejection are insecurity and low self esteem. The enemy would have you to believe that you will never be accepted. So many people have been diagnosed as manic depressive and take all kinds of medication. Once the devil gets a grip on your mind, he'll try to destroy you. He'll even go as far as having you consider suicide. You see, it's very serious. But being a child of the living God you have protection. You have the powerful hand of God and His love to keep you. You can run safely to His arms.

There is a cure for the fear of rejection. Trusting in God's love for you. That is the cure. You should never believe that your self-worth depends on another person. God loves you unconditionally. Daniel 10:19 says, *"Don't be afraid, for you are deeply loved by God. Be at peace, take heart and be strong."* Then Psalms 56:11 goes on to say, *"I trust in God, so I will not be afraid. What can people do to me?"* Jesus was pierced in His side on Calvary to take the pain of your inner hurts. Allow that healing to take place in your life today. Once you accept that love you must go one step further to complete your journey to overcoming. You must give yourself away to someone else in a similar situation. We can't see the pain of others when we dwell on our own. But when you are helping someone else conquer their fears, you become so strong and fearless! It's like self therapy. God's love will flow through you to another person, while strengthening you to be a warrior against the very thing that tried to destroy you. Isn't He amazing?! Praise Him now!

MY PRAYER: WEEK 18

Father God, I come to you today thanking you for delivering me from the fear of rejection. I no longer have to find acceptance from others because I know that you love me unconditionally. Thank you for healing my inner hurts and broken heart. Thank you for allowing me to run to you being assured that no one could love me more than you. Give me the strength and direction to help others overcome the same fear that I successfully conquered. In Jesus' name, amen.

MY SCRIPTURES

Psalms 27:1, 1 John 4:18, Ephesians 1:4,
Psalms 27:10, 2 Corinthians 10:18

MY CHALLENGE: WEEK 18

Overcoming the fear of rejection can be quite difficult, if you're doing it on your own. This is something you must call on God to help you do. Study these scriptures and read them aloud to yourself. Be sure to stick with your prayer plan, talking to God several times a day. The close relationship with Him will be the power you need to succeed. The Enemy cannot come between you and God, no matter how he tries.

Your challenge for this week is to face that fear of rejection. God has not given you the spirit of fear. There may be a friend, family member, neighbor, or co-worker in your life who may not feel accepted or loved like God wants them to be. This is your chance to become a warrior against rejection! Take some time to shower them with love. Take that person to lunch or for a walk in the park. Let them know that God loves them unconditionally and He sent you to show them just how special they are. God will deliver YOU as you reach out to help someone else overcome the same challenge!

If you think of some things you wished someone would have said or done when you were in the dumps, do those things for this person. I promise you the joy in your heart will grow into so much strength for you and that person. Share this lesson with them. Pray with them. Give them a Godly hug and tell them everything is going to be alright. You must be the hands of God in their life.

MY PERSONAL JOURNAL

WEEK 18

MY GOALS:

MY ACCOMPLISHMENTS:

19 ~ TEMPORARY PLEASURES

"By faith Moses, when he was grown up, refused to be called the son of Pharaoh's daughter, choosing rather to be mistreated with the people of God than to enjoy the fleeting pleasures of sin. He considered the reproach of Christ greater wealth than the treasures of Egypt, for he was looking to the reward. By faith he left Egypt, not being afraid of the anger of the king, for he endured as seeing Him who is invisible." (Hebrews 11:24-27)

Sin is the disease that keeps us away from God. The Enemy knows this and so do you. It comes in many forms. Sin can be obvious or discreet. It can hurt openly or feel very good. Whatever the case - sin is still sin, and it will separate you from God.

As a child of God you must be very careful not to fall into the traps of the Enemy. The word tell us exactly what his goal is in John 10:10, *"The thief cometh not but that he may steal, kill, and destroy: I came that they may have life, and have it abundantly."* Knowing this, you must realize that when that devil comes, he won't look like a red monster with a tail and horns. He will come as the very thing you desire. These things are sins in the form of temporary pleasures.

God gives us many blessings daily. When we use the blessings of God in a way that does not bring Him glory, we sin. He will curse every abused gift and since it brings only temporary pleasure, it will bring horrible consequences. Gluttony, sexual promiscuity, drunkenness, and greed are some examples of what sin can do when we fail to use His gifts in the way they were intended. Sin is very pleasurable, or there would not be addictions. When you disconnect your search for pleasure from Father God, then the Devil becomes the father or ruler of your life. This is the reason he refers to us as "dead in transgressions and sins" in Ephesians 2:1. Your sins will cut you off from the

Source of spiritual life like a plant being disconnected from its roots. God's blessings must be used for His intention and service or they become a curse.

There is good news, it's not too late! Today you can be reconciled to God. He sent Jesus Christ to pay the penalty of your sins. Not only that, He has given you promises that are trustworthy. Psalms 16:11 says, *"You will show me the path of life; in your presence is fullness of joy; at your right hand are pleasures forever more."* David said in Psalms 36:8 that God's people "are abundantly satisfied with the fullness of your house, and you give them drink from the river of your pleasures." If you keep the kingdom of God first in all you do, He will give you all the other things you desire, according to His will. (Matthew 6:33)

Don't allow sin to cut off your spiritual lifeline. Be aware of the tactics of the Enemy and don't fall for them. There is a great reward for those that stay faithful to the will of God. More than you could ever imagine!

MY PRAYER: WEEK 19

Dear Heavenly Father, I come to you today asking for forgiveness from all my sins. Even though I have confessed Jesus as my Lord and Savior, I sometimes fall short of what I should be in your sight. I want to be clean. I want to be whole. Fill me with your Spirit that I may withstand the works of the enemy. Help me as I face temptations. You promised to give me the power to overcome temptation and I now walk with the confidence that I can and will turn away from sin. Thank you for reconciliation. Thank you for your grace and mercy that follows me every day of my life. In Jesus' name I pray, amen.

MY SCRIPTURES

1 Timothy 6:17-19, Romans 1:20-21, Luke 12:13-21, Matthew 25:30-31,46, Revelation 21:6-7, 22:17

MY CHALLENGE: WEEK 19

As we cover the topic of sin this week, I don't want to focus on the obvious. (We all know stealing, killing, adultery, etc. are obvious.) I want you to take a look at your life and see if you can detect the sly tactics of the enemy using the blessings that God has given you to cause you to sin.

Are you spending more time bragging about that new house than you are bragging about God blessing you with it? Are you driving that new car everywhere under the sun except to church services or to witness to others? What about that refrigerator? Is it filled with foods that cause you to overeat? Are you wearing that low-cut dress to try to catch a man's eye? Are you using that new cell phone to call someone you shouldn't be calling? Are you texting the wrong types of messages? What are you watching late at night?

This week is "clean sweep" week. It's time to clean up your life. You are a child of God and your life should show that. It doesn't matter if no one sees what you're doing or hears what you're saying. GOD DOES. The Holy Spirit who lives in you has been hurt by what you hide. Now would be a great time to get serious with God about your spiritual life. He has so many promises waiting for you. All the devil has is death and hell..

If you don't remember anything else, remember this: Romans 6:23 "The wages of sin is death, but the Gift of God is eternal life through Jesus Christ our Lord."

Payday will surely come. What will be your reward?

MY PERSONAL JOURNAL

WEEK 19

MY GOALS:

MY ACCOMPLISHMENTS:

20 ~ EARTHLY TREASURES

"But store up for yourselves treasures in heaven, where neither moth nor rust destroys, and where thieves do not break in or steal; for where your treasure is, there your heart will be also." (Matthew 6:20-21)

Name the five most valuable things in your life. That answer would be very different depending on who you ask. A rich, healthy person's answers would be totally different from a person laying in intensive care breathing their last breath. A comfortable housewife's answer would be different from a successful single mother. The simple truth is, we all have "things" that we place great value upon. But do we place too much value in these things?

We live in a society today where success is measured by material possessions, education level, GPA, accomplishments, power, fame, and especially fortune. There is nothing at all wrong with any of these things when placed in a Godly perspective. God desires that we prosper. In fact the bible teaches us about people who were very prosperous and had many treasures, but they didn't allow them to destroy their relationship with Him. come between. Abraham was very wealthy, yet he was still called *"a friend of God"* in 2 Chronicles 20:7. Job would have been a multi-millionaire in today's world. He had a great home, career, and family. He owned a huge farm, 500 oxen plowing the fields and 500 donkeys taking his produce to market. That would be 500 tractors for the field and 500 trucks today! He developed a large transportation company with 3,000 camels (buses today). And he had employees to work ALL of this.

You see, treasures are not bad. They are actually blessings of the Lord. Where the problem comes in is when you place more value on these things than you do on your eternal life in heaven. It's time to take inventory and do a little damage control. Things that tie you to the world can risk your losing eternal life.

So what are the heavenly treasures you need to value more than your material possessions? I'm glad you asked. You need to keep a stock-pile of these treasures: compassion, generosity, love, humility, kindness, sympathy, patience, and obedience to Father God. These treasures will measure the greatness of a person in the eyes of God. They tell who a person really is. As you account for all the most valuable things in your life, be thankful for them. Let God know that you realize that He alone is your source and you would never place any of it above Him. Keeping material things in their perspective place will not only lead to more success and blessings, but it will ensure your place in heaven. Material blessings should be a tool used for the glory of God. You're blessed to be a blessing.

MY PRAYER: WEEK 20

Father God, today I thank you for all blessings you have given me. Forgive me if I have ever placed anything above my heavenly treasures. You alone are my source and provider. Nothing I gain is due to my own provision. Help me to keep my priorities in order. Use me to be a blessing to others. Let my success and provision through your mercy and grace be an opportunity for me to bring glory to You. I will always give you honor and praise and let others know that all good things come from above. Lord I know that material things will one day be gone, but my life will face an eternity. Help me to ensure that my eternity is with You. In Jesus' name, amen.

MY SCRIPTURES

Hebrews 11:13-16, Matthew 6:19-24, 1 Peter 1:3-6,
1 Corinthians 3:12-15, Exodus 20:3, Luke 18:17-23 Job Chapter 1

MY CHALLENGE: WEEK 20

Earthly treasures can easily take top priority in your life if you are not careful. Most of the time we don't even realize it. We boast about a new house or car, never giving God glory. We flaunt a new diamond ring to our friends, hoping they get jealous. We get new furniture, but don't want anyone to sit on it. We buy expensive clothes so we can be the "star of the show". Is this going to get you into the kingdom? Is this becoming of a Christian? Certainly not!

This week is inventory week. We all have some personal treasure. It may not be expensive. If you're homeless it may be a cart. If you're in college, it may be a new computer. It may be money, clothes, yard equipment, or whatever. You get the drift. We all have "stuff" that we love and treasure. Make a list of your treasures and sincerely thank God for them. Ask Him to show you how you can use your earthly treasures to His glory. It may be as simple as telling someone that GOD blessed you with this...and you could never have gotten it on your own!

Secondly, look at the heavenly treasures listed in the devotion: compassion, generosity, love, humility, kindness, sympathy, patience, and obedience. Challenge yourself to allow every one of them to become a characteristic that you strive to acquire on a daily basis. Let these traits become who you are. If you seek after these treasures with all your heart, then you will be securing your eternity with God.

MY PERSONAL JOURNAL

WEEK 20

MY GOALS:

MY ACCOMPLISHMENTS:

21 ~ FROM ADDICTION TO DEVOTION

"Do you not know that when you present yourselves to someone as slaves for obedience, you are slaves of the one you obey, either of sin resulting in death, or of obedience? But thanks be to God that though you were slaves of sin, you became obedient from the heart to that form of teaching to which you were committed, and having been freed from sin, you became slaves of righteousness." (Romans 6: 16-18)

Addiction and devotion are very similar, yet very different. The definition of addiction is stated as being the condition of being habitually or compulsively occupied with or involved in something that could ultimately destroy you. Devotion is said to be having a great interest in something to which a large portion of your time is devoted.

The chains of addiction are usually too small to be felt until it's too late or too strong for you to overcome without help. The source of the addiction becomes the master, and you become the slave. The end consequences of feeding a habit can destroy your dreams and literally assassinate your ambitions.

From time to time, everyone struggles with some sort of bad habit or addiction. The difference between a habit and an addiction is that a habit is something you do often, but you can stop it at anytime. An addiction is actually loss of control over an act. You cannot stop it at will. If you need a cup of coffee everyday in order to function, you're addicted. If you choose to have a cup of coffee in the morning, but you can really do without it and not lose your mind...that would be a habit. All addiction is sinful.

God has given us free will whether to subject ourselves to bad habits and addictions or to devote our lives to Him. In order to avoid or overcome addictions, we must submit ourselves to the Holy Spirit and walk by the Spirit. One of the fruits of the spirit is self-control. We are able to walk by the Spirit because we belong to Christ. Therefore as Christians we have the power to control our bodies by having the mind of Christ in us.

There are some strongholds that cannot be broken without help. If you find yourself in bondage from addiction, ask for God to forgive you and find a Gospel-preaching pastor or minister to pray with you until you get a breakthrough. Get spiritual counseling and devote yourself to God completely. There is deliverance directly from heaven available for you.

Once you've overcome be sure to devote more time to studying His word and walk in obedience to it so that you won't be subject to fall again to that stronghold. The enemy will use your weakness to destroy your relationship with God. Oh but greater is He that is in you, than he that is in the world! You are more than a conqueror through Christ Jesus! You have the power of the living God on your side and no weapon formed against you shall prosper! Walk in victory!

MY PRAYER: WEEK 21

Dear Heavenly Father, I want to thank you for loving me enough to pull me up out of the turmoil of addiction. Lord I can't overcome by myself, I need your powerful hand. Forgive me of my sin. Clean my heart from all the addictive sins that cause me to separate from your will. Place a desire for devotion to your will and your word in my soul. Give me the power to hold on to my deliverance and to walk in authority over all evil powers that try to come up against me. Nothing can separate me from your love. Thank you for delivering me! I will live a devoted life for your glory. In Jesus' name, amen.

MY SCRIPTURES

Romans 1:16, 1 Thessalonians 2:13, 1 Peter 3:12, Galatians 2:20, Galatians 5:24, Philippians 4:13, 1 John 4:4, Romans 8:31-39

MY CHALLENGE: WEEK 21

Some people judge others as "bad sinners" when they have drug or sex addictions. The truth is, all addiction is sin. Anything that has power over your mind and causes you to do things that keep you out of Father's will needs to be banished from your life.

In order to release these strongholds from your life you must first acknowledge the fact that you have a problem. This week I want you to check yourself for habits or addictions. Anything that has control over your mind that is not Christ must be dealt with. You may be addicted to food. If so, work on a diet plan. It may be smoking, if so then work on quitting. Maybe it's shopping to the point of excessive debt. My dear, it's time to take control over your life.

Find your bad habits and lay them on the altar. Make it a priority to give the Holy Spirit control over your mind and body. Once you've overcome, be sure to testify of your success. Your testimony will be strength for someone else.

If your addiction is beyond your control, I pray that you will seek professional help as well as spiritual counseling. It's to your benefit to protect the Spirit of Christ who dwells within. He cannot live in an unclean temple. It's up to you to prepare a comfortable place for Him to live. I know you can overcome your addiction and turn it into total devotion to God. All your help comes from Him. He is willing if you are ready. If you need professional help, please get it. But always hold on to God through the process. He is your ultimate key to total deliverance.

MY PERSONAL JOURNAL

WEEK 21

MY GOALS:

MY ACCOMPLISHMENTS:

22 ~ DEALING WITH GUILT

"For all have sinned and fall short of the glory of God, and are justified by His grace as a gift, through the redemption that is in Christ Jesus." (Romans 3:23-24)

Guilt can be a very heavy burden, too heavy for you to carry. It is a spiritual oppression that keeps you from forgiving yourself of the wrongs you've done to yourself or to someone else. The Enemy will use guilt to make you think that God will not forgive you or that you are not worthy of His forgiveness. Remember, the devil is the master of lies!

Overcoming guilt is a personal decision you alone must make. When it tries to overtake you, quote the scripture above. Get it down in your spirit. The blood that Jesus shed on the Cross was for your redemption. He took all that guilt to the cross for you.

Fighting guilt can be a battle, but the word of God is the weapon you need to defeat the Enemy. Study Hebrews 10:17-23. Let's break it on down right here. God says He will not remember your sins anymore. He means it! He won't throw your past up in your face to make you suffer He's already forgiven you for. Your past was washed away the moment He forgave you. Gone forever! Verse 18 reminds you that you cannot pay for the wrong you've done. Once Jesus shed His blood, it was paid in full. Every sin you ever committed or will commit has already been covered by the blood. Once you repent, you are washed clean again. Verse 20 lets you know that in the days of old, the priest would be a mediator between you and God. But since Jesus was sacrificed, there is no priest needed. He was the ultimate sacrifice and Mediator between you and God.

You are now privileged to draw near to God with a sincere heart. You can be assured through faith that God will forgive your sins and wash away all guilt from your life. He is faithful to His promises. No longer should you ever feel guilty about anything that you've released to God for forgiveness. The key here is to repent.

Father God is not like man. He is true to His word. One of the biggest lies the Devil will try to get you to believe is that the cross is only for the forgiven Christians. Not true! Luke 5:32 reminds you that Jesus said, "I came not to call the righteous, but the sinner to repentance." The cross is for the sinner! John 3:17 says, "For God sent not His son into the world to condemn the world; but that the world through Him might be saved."

Before you allow the Devil to whisper lies in your ear and convince you into believing that you are not worthy of forgiveness, get into the word of God and denounce all negative thoughts with the promises of God. Whatever you did wrong, take it to God and claim your deliverance. Repent and walk into victory!

MY PRAYER: WEEK 22

Father God, thank you for keeping every promise in your word. Forgive me for harboring guilt in my heart and allowing it to eat away at my mind. I know I've done wrong and I confess it to you now. I repent right now. Cleanse me from the stains of sin in my life. I've learned from my mistakes. I will no longer carry the burden of guilt of sin over my life. Guilt has no control over me any longer. I am free in Jesus' name, amen.

MY SCRIPTURES

Hebrews 10:17-23, Romans 8:1, John 8:36, 1 John 1:9

MY CHALLENGE: WEEK 22

When we have accepted Jesus into our lives we are new creations. There is such a clean, healthy feeling inside that is like no other. But even though we are saved, we must remember that we are still human by nature. If we take our eyes off God for just a slight moment, the enemy will find that weak spot in our hearts and cause us to sin. Father God knew this would happen. That is the purpose for Jesus being sacrificed on the cross. It wasn't just for your initial salvation. It was to pardon every sin that you may commit AFTER your salvation!

Your challenge for this week is to look within your heart and address anything that may be causing you to carry a burden of guilt. You might have said or done something that hurt someone. Maybe you caused someone to get into trouble. It could be that you told a lie on someone and now you wish you never said those words. Your guilt may be even greater than any of these. Just remember that Jesus paid the price for your redemption.

Take your guilty burdens to God in prayer. Ask for forgiveness and repent. Refrain from doing it ever again. Now allow the love of God to give you that "clean" feeling again. You are refreshed and renewed in Christ. This is a chance for you to give Him praise! His love for you is unconditional. It's up to you to make the choice to accept His forgiveness. Don't let the sacrifice that Jesus made be in vain. Take it personal because it was for you.

MY PERSONAL JOURNAL

WEEK 22

MY GOALS:

MY ACCOMPLISHMENTS:

23 ~ CHOOSE LIFE

"I call heaven and earth as witnesses today against you, that I have set before you life and death, blessing and cursing; therefore choose life, that both you and your descendants may live." (Deuteronomy 30:19)
"I am the Way, the Truth, and the Life..." (John 14:6)

You were created with the privilege and responsibility to choose. God didn't create humans to be like puppets. It is your choice to choose to live your life for His glory and receive eternal life, or to live in sin which leads to eternal death and damnation. Your choice doesn't end there. If you place the two scriptures together, you'll see that God plainly let's you know that Jesus is your life choice. By choosing Him, you will definitely live. Not only you, but your descendents as well! But there is more to it than simply accepting Jesus as your Savior.

There are many Christians who accept Christ into their lives and stop at that point. They just want to make it into heaven. Here is a newsflash for you. You were called to be disciples and follow after Jesus examples. It is your duty to live a purposeful life here on earth even before you get to heaven. How do you do that? I'm so glad you asked. If you remember from chapter 8 you learned that there is a purpose for your life. In order to live a life that is filled with the glory of God, you must birth what He placed in you. Once you are given the gift of eternal life, you must make it a priority to follow the plans that God has made for you to bring life to others. By following His instructions, you are not only pleasing Him, you are doing what it takes to bring life to your descendants. God promises that.

Don't just accept Jesus and become stale and stagnant, waiting on Him to return. You are more than that. You are blessed with ability and purpose to add to the Kingdom of God. When you decide to step into your divine calling, you may be nervous or even questionable about what to do. Trust God. He will order your steps and guide you through. Be obedient to His will. Good deeds, fasting, giving, praising, helping in your church are all good works, but obedience is better than sacrifice (1 Samuel 15:22). Obey what He is leading you to do for the Kingdom. There are so many promises and rewards for doing His will.

Today I am encouraging you to choose life. Don't abort what God has placed inside you to do for the Kingdom. Jesus is life. Choosing Him doesn't just mean accepting Him as Savior. It means taking up your cross and following Him. Do what He did. Reach out to the world around you and offer this same life to a hurting and dying society. Your calling may not be for multitudes, but it's for somebody. Bring the promise of life to your descendants by walking in obedience to God's plan for your life. I promise you, there will be a great reward in heaven for your choice.

MY PRAYER: WEEK 23

Heavenly Father, thank you for giving me the privilege to choose. Thank you not only for the freedom of choice, but for giving me a divine purpose to help others choose as well. Forgive me for not completely stepping into my purpose. I need your guidance. Speak to me, Lord and show me what to do for the Kingdom. I am willing to do your will and I place my all feelings aside. Remove any distractions, hindrances, and obstacles out of my way so that I may hear you clearly. Call forth my anointing in the name of Jesus, amen.

MY SCRIPTURES

Proverbs 3:5, Romans 8:29, 11:33, Genesis 12:1, Hebrews 11:8

MY CHALLENGE: WEEK 23

Sometimes as Christians we can get comfortable doing nothing other than attending weekly church services. Eventually you'll find yourself even slacking in that area. Taking your salvation for granted is very dangerous. When you don't do anything to keep your spirit alive, it will get weak and eventually die. Your weakness becomes a perfect target for the enemy. Soon after that, you'll find yourself back in your old ways, hanging with your old crowd, and sin takes over. The Spirit of God cannot and will not dwell in an unclean temple.

This week you are going to make a choice. You can choose to remain stagnant in your spiritual life and risk losing your eternal life with Jesus, or you can choose to make your discipleship the priority in your life. You can choose to stay comfortable with what you are doing now for Christ, or you can choose to make yourself available for God to use you for His glory and building up the Kingdom. No matter what you are doing now, you can always increase. Your Christian life is all about growth. You can't stay the same size. This week you can choose life, or choose to abort!

MY PERSONAL JOURNAL

WEEK 23

MY GOALS:

MY ACCOMPLISHMENTS:

24 ~ GRIEF

"Be merciful to me Lord, for I am in distress; my eyes grow weak with sorrow, my soul and body with grief." (Psalms 31:9)

The loss of a loved one is one of the hardest pains to deal with and overcome. Letting go can be painful both mentally and physically. You feel as if your whole world is crashing down around you. There is sadness, anger, unanswered questions, and emptiness. It seems like there are more emotions than you can bear.

After the loss and grief, there is still the mourning process. That first year that follows is the hardest. The first birthday, anniversary, holiday, or maybe you planned something that you'll never get to see happen. The pain of grief is definitely overwhelming. Thank God for His grace and mercy. He knew you'd have these days. That's why He created tear ducts for your tears to channel outwardly. While you're releasing the pain and shedding those tears, He is healing you on the inside.

Getting through the healing process can be tough. This is a time to trust God and allow the healing to take place naturally. When those special days come around, talk about the good times you shared with your loved one. Revisit the good times and memories. Laugh your heart out! The best way to deal with pain is to find your joy again. This is where your strength develops. There will be sunshine after your storm. Understand that it is normal to feel the pain several years after your loss. Just know that your Heavenly Father will comfort and strengthen you to make it through it all.

Even though grief is painful, there are some good things that come out of healthy grief. You probably can't see it during your process, but you'll realize the good soon. You'll have a new perspective on life and see things differently. You'll place more value on life. Things that you have taken for granted will now be important. You'll long for heaven like never before. It becomes more tangible now that you can envision your loved one living there. You draw closer to God because you can sense there is really nowhere else you can turn. His love becomes more real than ever to you.

Use your grieving process to strengthen your relationship with your Heavenly Father. He cares for you. He comforts you. It's such a good feeling to know that you can wake up in the middle of the night and talk to Him and know that He's alert and ready to hear from you. Cry now if you must. Scream, yell, weep. It's all a part of releasing your pain. It's the outward expression of your inward pain. God understands and He will always be right there. Soon you'll be strong enough to laugh again and find joy in your sorrow. God has never left you alone, and He's not about to leave you when you need Him most!

MY PRAYER: WEEK 24

My God, my Father...I need your comfort now. Help me to find peace in the middle of this storm. I cannot bear this pain alone. I have so many questions, so much pain, and I am weak. Only you can hear my cry and understand my pain. Father God, I love you more than words can say. You know the brokenness of my heart. Heal me from the inside. Mend all the shattered pieces. Help me to find strength in You. I know that in time it will get better. Until then, help me to be able to look to You for peace and understanding. In Jesus' name I pray, amen.

MY SCRIPTURES

Psalms 34:17-18, Psalms 63:1, 2 Corinthians 12:9, Philippians 4:13, Matthew 5:4, 1 Samuel 16:7, Ecclesiastes 3:4

MY CHALLENGE: WEEK 24

Grief alone is a challenge. It would be insensitive to ask you to go through a grieving process as an assignment. What I would like you to do is take time this week to talk to Father God about your own personal losses. We've all experienced them in some way or another. Find comfort in knowing that He will be there to wipe away your tears and fill that void in your heart with His love and comfort.

If you know someone who is now grieving over the loss of a loved one, be there for them. Don't ask any questions. Don't offer any personal advise. Just be there to listen to their stories and memories. Cook or purchase a meal, do a few chores, or run any errands they may need. Just make yourself available. There is no loneliness like that of the death of a loved one. This is your chance to be the hands and arms of God. Showing compassion and love is one of the greatest things you can do. Use this opportunity wisely.

MY PERSONAL JOURNAL

WEEK 24

MY GOALS:

MY ACCOMPLISHMENTS:

25 ~ OVERLOOKED AND UNAPPRECIATED

"He told them, "A prophet has little honor in his hometown, among his relatives, on the streets he played as a child." Jesus wasn't able to do much of anything there - he laid hands on a few sick people and healed them, that's all." (Mark 6:4-6)

Does this sound familiar? God puts a dream in your heart and you do everything according to His will to bring it to life. Your anointing is great. You are a blessing to so many people. Then life gets real. Your family talks badly about you. They belittle your anointing and even say hurtful things to your face. The people who should have your back have turned away from you. The very ones who you thought would support you are not there at all. The same thing happened to Jesus. As you've read in the scripture, when Jesus was in His hometown He couldn't work as powerful in the anointing because of the lack of faith from his family and friends.

When God calls you to do a work for Him, stay faithful to Him. There is a purpose in your calling. The ridicule can be very painful and even embarrassing at times, but you continue on anyway. You must work as unto the Lord. It's not about what "they" may think or say. It's about you being faithful to your faithful God. He will vindicate you in the end.

1 Corinthians chapter 12 reminds us that we are all part of the body of Christ. We all have a job to do and each one is important. Don't ever allow the opinions of family and friends determine your worth in the Kingdom of God. Your purpose is very valuable and you are worth more than fine jewels to your Heavenly Father. See yourself through His eyes. His work through you is great, no matter what it is.

You may not be educated in the field that God called you into. You may not speak like Billy Graham, but God gave you a message for somebody to hear. God doesn't call the qualified, He qualifies the ones He calls. So let them keep talking. You'll live through the pain and insults. When your blessings start pouring in, God will get the last laugh, and so will you. Your faithfulness is what God sees. Continue to walk upright before Him. Feed your faith in the word and know that He is with you. He didn't leave you in the wilderness to die. Your purpose will bring hope and life to the very ones who are against you right now.

1 Peter says, *"Humble yourselves therefore, under God's mighty hand, that He may lift you up in due time."* No matter what God called you to do, you won't start out on top. You must grow and take it step by step. It's "on the job training" in many cases. Just remember that if He called you to do it, He will lead you all the way through it. Your day at the top is coming if you stay faithful and follow His will. Great will be your reward. "They" can't stop what God has started in your life.

MY PRAYER: WEEK 25

Father God, thank you for using me in a great way. My availability to you has opened so many doors for my life. I realize that my purpose was predestined by You, and that I am qualified to do my assignment. My worth is not determined by my family, friends, or anyone else. Use me for the Kingdom and to bring glory to Your name. I will stay strong! I will obey your word! I will endure, no matter who doesn't support me. As long as I have you on my side, I can make it. In Jesus name, amen.

MY SCRIPTURES

1 Corinthians 12:12-27, Romans 12:4-5, 1 Peter 5:6

MY CHALLENGE: WEEK 25

Once you know what your purpose or calling is, the enemy will use everything in his little mind to destroy it. He knows who to use and what to make them say to try to discourage you. Thank God you know his little tactics and have the whole armor of God.

This week take a look at your purpose and see how you can gain ground for the Kingdom. God is ready to expand your territory. What can you do to keep up with this expansion? You're growing into a greater anointing and now you must do more than usual to keep up with that growth.

Secondly, once you pinpoint what you need to do be sure to increase your prayer time. Seek God for direction. Never make any decisions, especially Kingdom decisions, without God's approval. He will tell you exactly what's next. He will open more doors, and close some as well. Be prepared for change. Remember, the higher go, the thinner the air will get. Elevation sometimes causes separation. As you go higher, there will be people talking about you, walking away from you, and your support system may fall away. Just keep your focus on God.

This is a great time to stretch your faith. You'll need it during this season. Hang onto His hands and don't let go!

MY PERSONAL JOURNAL

WEEK 25

MY GOALS:

MY ACCOMPLISHMENTS:

26 ~ SCARS OF LIFE

"But He was wounded for our transgressions, He was bruised for our iniquities: the chastisement of our peace was upon Him; and by His stripes we are healed." (Isaiah 53:5)

Isn't it amazing how little boys like to compare their scars with other little boys? I guess they want to see who's tougher. We all have a scar or two. Some are visible due to accidents, injuries, surgeries, or fights. But then there are the invisible scars that no one can see with the eye. They can be the most painful. Whether they are inward or outward scars, they all have a story.

The evidence of what you've been through is identified by a scar. You may be proud of your scar, or you may be very hurt to reveal it. When God created man, I'm sure that he caused scars to remain in our lives for a reason. That reason is not intended for you to use your past pain as an excuse to be a victim. You are victorious, an over-comer, and more than a conqueror. If you allow God to heal you completely from whatever caused the scar, you will see a purpose in the pain. He'll turn your scars into stars, using them to help someone else heal.

Think about this amazing fact: Jesus used the scars of His wounds from the crucifixion to identify Himself to the disciples after the resurrection. He certainly didn't have to keep those scars when He was raised. It was His divine choice. They were signs to His people to remind them of His love (Isaiah 49:16). They showed that He went through torment so that we may live. Those beautiful scars mean life to you today.

The 39 stripes on Jesus back were for the 39 categories of sickness and disease that could make you sick or kill you. He was pierced in the side for all your inward pains. He was bruised to cover the curses passed down from generations to you. You see, scars are not intended to hold you back. They are reminders of what the Lord has brought you out of and what He gave you strength to conquer. There is no pain that He cannot feel and no scar that He cannot heal.

Bring all those ugly scars to your Savior. Even the secret ones that haven't quite healed yet. Place them in His nail scarred hands and allow Him to make you whole. He suffered so that you can walk free from all sorrow. You don't have to cover the pain any longer. You cannot continue to live as a victim. All you have to do is call on the name of Jesus and He will fix all the broken pieces. One touch from the Master will change your life. Your healing is vital in the Kingdom. There are people out there hurting beyond what they can handle. Your victory will strengthen their faith and give them hope in Jesus. Be healed in Jesus' name!

MY PRAYER: WEEK 26

Dear Father God, thank you for the sacrifice of Jesus Christ and the scars He carries to remind me of Your love for me. I have so many scars, Some visible and many invisible. Forgive me for not letting go and allowing You to heal all my hurts. Today I lay them before You. I cannot carry them any longer. I accept the healing that Jesus carried to the cross for my sake. Make me whole in Jesus' name, amen.

MY SCRIPTURES

Luke 24:36-53, Isaiah 49:16, Romans 5:8

MY CHALLENGE: WEEK 26

We all have been hurt. Whether it be physically, emotionally, or spiritually, pain is pain. Some things we can quickly get over, like a silly disagreement or stubbed toe. But there are many times we carry hurts within ourselves for years. Some of those inner hurts even have visible outward scars. I am so glad to be able to be a witness to you that Jesus can heal it all!

This week talk to God about your scars. Show them to Him one by one. He can see even the deepest wounds that no one else can see or cares to see. Your wholeness is so important to Him. Open yourself up this week and allow His air to touch your wounded heart. You deserve to be free. You deserve to be happy again. Let it all go! Healing is yours.

Promise the Lord that you won't use the scars of your past to limit what you do for Him. No more crutches, no more bandages, no more excuses. You are completely made whole! In Jesus' name! Go and be free!!

MY PERSONAL JOURNAL

WEEK 26

MY GOALS:

MY ACCOMPLISHMENTS:

27 ~ INFERTILITY: THE MISSING PIECE

"...neither let the eunuch say, Behold, I am a dry tree." (Isaiah 56:3) "Even to them will I give in my house and within my walls a place and a name better than of sons and of daughters: I will give them an everlasting name, that shall not be cut off." (Isaiah 56:5)

Infertility can be very heart-breaking to both men and women. You see other people having children every day. You read about others abusing their children and wonder why God would allow them to have the gift of parenthood. Receiving the news from your doctor that you will never be able to conceive can be very similar to grieving the loss of a loved one. In biblical days the word "eunuch" was used to describe ones who were not able to bare children. Matthew 9:12 teaches us that some eunuchs were born that way, some were made that way (castrated) by others, and some chose to be that way. In modern times you would apply this teaching to be people born or have become infertile, people who have undergone surgery to prevent children (vasectomy or tubal ligation), or people who choose to dedicate their lives to God and do not have sexual relations (nuns, monks, priests, etc.).

When dealing with infertility, desiring to have children can be overwhelming and painful. Take comfort in knowing that God knows your pain. Sounds simple doesn't it? This can be the hardest thing to apprehend during your time of despair. Being a parent is not an assignment given to everyone. Even though it may be your heart's desire, it may not be God's will. And if it is His will, you must trust and believe that He will allow it to happen in His perfect time. Some people are placed here to be adoptive parents, some are to be teachers to children, some will be mentors, etc. Use this time to build your relationship with

Father God. Ask Him what His will is for your life concerning children. Above all, be willing to accept the answer. You must take today's scripture to heart and hear God saying, "You are not damaged goods."

He has a very special blessing for you if you devote your life to Him and trust in His word. That's what He promised. Your challenge is to endure and know that there is a reason for it all. As you go through this time there are four things you should do: 1. Lay your doubts, emotions, and frustrations at His feet. 2. Listen to His voice in your quiet prayer time. 3. Ask God to give you eyes to see the blessing in this burden. 4. Ask for prayer from your pastor and other church leaders or friends. Build your faith and God will make your test a testimony. There may be a miracle child waiting, there may be many other blessings coming through you to help many children. Just trust God let His will be done. You're blessed!

<u>MY PRAYER: WEEK 27</u>

Father God, hear the cry from my broken heart. I am so burdened with possible infertility. I know that you created me and nothing is impossible for you. I believe by the power in the blood of Jesus Christ, I am made whole and complete. You have given children to barren couples so many times in your word. I believe that I am the next miracle parent. I have no doubt that if I continue to walk in your will, living uprightly before you, there is healing assigned to me. Do for me what you did for Abraham and Sarah, for Isaac and Rebekah, for Rachel and Jacob, for Manoah and his wife, for Hannah and Elkanah, and so many more. Let your will be done in my life. Use my situation for your glory. I give you all the praise. I claim deliverance and I accept your will in my life. I will forever trust you. Let your spirit rest in me. In Jesus' name, amen.

MY SCRIPTURES

Genesis 17:15-21, 18:9-15, 15:6, Hebrews 11:11,
Genesis 25:21, Genesis 30:22,24
Judges 13:3,12
1 Samuel 2:21, 2 Kings 4:8-17, Luke Chapter 1
Psalms 84:11, Psalms 113:9

MY CHALLENGE: WEEK 27

Infertility is a challenge of its own. Having faith to be delivered from it is even greater. If you are facing this battle, I encourage you today to build your faith strong and unstoppable. Study the scriptures for this week and let the stories of conquering infertility take root in your soul. I am believing God with you for a great manifestation of His glorious power.

Everyone is not facing infertility in a natural sense. Maybe you are experiencing spiritual infertility. The Enemy has your mind burdened with thoughts that you will never be able to do what God has called you to do. This week I declare with you that the seed of purpose that God placed inside your heart will flourish!! You are about to give birth to that dream, that ministry, or that assignment!

This week is name your seed week. Call it out. Tell the Enemy that you have been infertile far too long. PUSH...Pray Until Something Happens!!!

MY PERSONAL JOURNAL

WEEK 27

MY GOALS:

MY ACCOMPLISHMENTS:

28 ~ G.I.C.U.

"Therefore humble yourselves under the mighty hand of God, that He may exalt you in due time, casting all your cares upon Him, for He cares for you." (1 Peter 5:6-7)

When people are critically ill they are sometimes placed in the Medical Intensive Care Unit (M.I.C.U.) or the Surgical Intensive Care Unit (S.I.C.U.) Even babies and children have intensive care units (P.I.C.U and N.I.C.U.) There are hundreds of rooms in hospitals, but only the severely ill need intensive care. As children of God, you aren't exempt from being critically ill spiritually. You easily recover from some spiritual injuries. But what about those internal injuries that hurt you to the core? A fellow church member does something terrible to you. You've been disgraced before the church. A leader or church mentor did something to break trust with you. These injuries can place you in G.I.C.U. (God's Intensive Care Unit).

We will all experience hurt feelings and we will get over them. Just because you accepted Jesus as your Savior doesn't mean you're free from abuse, neglect, rejection, or any pain. But who do you go to when your spirit it completely crushed? You go to Father God. He's interested in anything concerning His children. If He knows the number of hairs on your head, you know He has to really love and care for you. God knows every tear you shed according to Psalms 56:8 and He's there to heal all those broken places in your heart. It's during those times of brokenness that He can show His pure love for you.

A broken spirit can cause you to feel as if God is so far away from you. Your prayers seem to hit the ceiling and bounce back. There's no one there to offer prayer and you feel like no one really cares about you. That's when you must get in the word and allow the Lord to speak to you and show you how much He cares. Proverbs 15:3 reminds you that God's eyes are everywhere, watching the good and the bad. But what I love most is knowing that when I'm at my lowest point, Jesus is praying for me! That's right, Jesus intercedes for you. (Read Hebrews 7:25 and Romans 8:34).

It's so good to know that when you are spiritually sick, weak, and can't quite get it together God is still there. It was good enough for me to know that Jesus died for my sins, but to know that He is also praying and interceding for me too...wow that's just awesome, isn't it?!! You should feel great knowing that there is a G.I.C.U. available for your critically ill spirit. No need to pull the plug on your spiritual life. Hold on just a little while longer and watch God restore your life. This is temporary. Your recovery is guaranteed if you stay in the care of Father God. And guess what. Your bill was already paid in full on Calvary! Take all your cares to Him and let the healing begin.

MY PRAYER: WEEK 28

Dear Heavenly Father, thank you for loving and caring for me like no one else ever could. Today I bring my broken spirit to you. There is no other place I can go for this healing. Mend all the pieces of my broken heart and make me whole again. Fill me with love and kindness again. Help me to move on as I forgive any wrongs that may have been done to me. I release myself from all pain and confusion. I give it all to you, Lord. Thank you Jesus for interceding for me. My strength is weak, but my faith is strong. Thank you for refreshing my spirit. Thank you for new life! In Jesus' name, amen.

MY SCRIPTURES

Psalms 8:4, Psalms 23:1, Psalms 121:3, Matthew 6:32, Matthew 10:30-31, Luke 15:20, Isaiah 49:15, Philippians 4:19, Proverbs 1:33, John 14:27

MY CHALLENGE: WEEK 28

Disappointments and pain are inevitable. There is just no way you will go through life without ever being emotionally hurt. As children of God we must learn to protect the Spirit that dwells within us. We must know that when that spiritual attack comes and we are hurt so deeply that we feel near death (spiritually), there is our God, right there to heal those injuries.

This week take some time to get a spiritual physical. Ask God to check you out real good and see if there is anything you need special care for. You may be holding some deep resentment towards someone. You may have something eating away at you that you need to forgive someone about so that it doesn't destroy you.

Our spiritual health is very important. Just as we have to get physical check-ups from time to time, we also need spiritual check-ups. Sometimes you don't know that there is anything wrong with you until you have The Physician take a look. Focus on a healthy spiritual lifestyle. Get healthy and stay healthy.

MY PERSONAL JOURNAL

WEEK: 28

MY GOALS:

MY ACCOMPLISHMENTS:

29 ~ PRISON OF TEMPTATION

"When tempted, no one should say, "God is tempting me." For God cannot be tempted by evil, nor does He tempt anyone. But each person is tempted when they are dragged away by their own evil desire and enticed. Then, after desire is conceived, it gives birth to sin; and sin, when it is full grown, gives birth to death." (James 1:13-15)

Once you accept Jesus as your Savior, you are a new creature. All things are passed away and new things have come. That's the word (2 Corinthians 5:17). But today we're going to talk about the temptation that separate you from God's presence. You know the one I'm talking about. That old habit that just keeps coming back no matter how hard you try to walk away from it. Why on earth can't I let this go? Is there something wrong with me? What am I doing wrong? Am I really saved? These are all common questions that come up when you have fallen to your old habits.

As long as you live, you will face some type of temptation. That's the Enemy's weapon to try to tear you away from God. Job 7:1 reminds us that *"The life of man upon earth is a warfare."* Temptations originate in your mind. Something will get your attention away from the word and hold onto it. Then you will begin to entertain it. That's when temptation turns into sin. If you entertain temptations, soon they will be entertaining you. Until you kill it from the root, it will always return. The key to conquering your temptation is getting your mind set on God and His word.

All temptations can be overcome through God (1 Corinthians 10:13). The way you respond to the attack of temptation will determine whether you stand with God or fall to sin. You have a choice whether or not to obey Him. It's during these times of testing by the enemy that you can and should become stronger in your faith. Just because you're saved doesn't mean your life will be smooth sailing. It's quite the opposite. You are in a battle for your soul. Keep your eyes on the prize of everlasting life. Know that there is nothing worth risking your eternal life in heaven for. Temptations are temporary pleasures, but heaven and hell are eternal.

Nip temptation in the bud and don't allow it to take root again. How can I fight it? Get in the word of God. Feed your spirit. Avoid situations that trigger ungodly desires. Recognize the source of your thoughts. Take control over them immediately, don't entertain trouble. Call on the Holy Spirit. He lives inside you, helping you fight the battle. This is the same Spirit that raised Christ from the dead, surely you know it can pull you away from falling to temptation. Finally, praise and worship Father God. The enemy has absolutely no power in His presence. That's where you need to stay.

MY PRAYER: WEEK 29

Heavenly Father, I want to thank you for loving me enough to give me power over temptation. Forgive me for the times that I didn't use that power, and I fell. I realize that what the devil used to destroy me has actually been turned around to strengthen me, humble me, and allowed you to purify me. Thank you for the Holy Spirit that gives me instructions during my times of testing. Keep a hedge of protection all around me. Temptation is only a test, and it will not destroy me. I have the victory in Jesus' name, amen.

MY SCRIPTURES

Romans 12:2, Ephesians 4:22-24, Philippians 4:8, Matthew 4:1-11

MY CHALLENGE: WEEK 29

Temptation is something we all have to confront at some point. It never just shows up once and leaves, it's a constant unwelcomed guest. Learning to keep your mind on God and keeping your focus on Godly things will help you fight it.

This week you will take note of any temptations that come to hinder your walk with God. Notice where the thoughts originated. What was your initial response to the thought? Thoughts conceive temptation and give birth to that sin! Once you learn the enemy's tactics for attracting you to certain weaknesses, you can know how to counter-attack.

After you identify the root of the temptation, take it to God in prayer. Ask for strength to resist it. Listen for direction and obey what God tells you to do. Remember, what may not bother some people can be destruction for you. Stay away from anything that may be the cause of your downfall.

Finally, always ask God to forgive you for the times you didn't resist temptation. You can always go to Him with a sincere heart and try again. Repentance is something you should never be afraid to seek. Father God wants you to be cleansed of all sin. Don't yield to temptation, drive by it as fast as possible!

MY PERSONAL JOURNAL

WEEK 29

MY GOALS:

MY ACCOMPLISHMENTS:

30 ~ PRIDE

"Do not love the world or the things in the world. If anyone loves the world, the love of the Father is not in him. For all that is in the world - the lust of the flesh, the lust of the eyes, and the pride of life - is not of the Father, but is of the world." (1 John 2:15-16)

I once knew a person who claimed to be a child of God. He was extremely prideful in every sense of the word. He always had to be the star of the show, the center of attention, and no one ever had anything better that he did (in his eyes). Where is he now? Suffering in anxiety and trying to hold on to everything he boasted about. Struggling to pay for all the material things he once bragged about. Lonely and depressed, drowning in sorrow, and trying to hide behind a mask of false prosperity.

Pride is one of the most dangerous sins to fall victim to. It is a puzzle with four pieces: selfishness, self-sufficiency, self-satisfaction, and self-esteem. Some may see pride as a virtue, but God sees it as an abomination (Proverbs 16:5) When we allow it to rule our lives, soon we no longer depend on Him. Once God is out of the equation, we become focused on our own ego. This is what causes God to turn away from us and allows the enemy to have easy access to our lives.

The sin of pride is what caused Lucifer to be cast out of Heaven. We should think of that example when our ego tries to rise up. You may not think you're better than God, but you may think you're better than anyone else. You may brag to people so much about what you've done or what you have that they feel inferior around you. Maybe they don't feel inferior, they just don't want to be around because of your boastful words. Being self-centered is a dangerous trait to possess. It can block your sense of repentance and permanently separate you from God if you allow it to.

There is a solution to dealing with pride. Humility is the answer. The bible teaches us how to put on humility: Philippians 2:2-4 tells us to consider others better than ourselves. James 4:7 reminds us to submit to the Lord by obeying His word. 2 Chronicles 34:27 says we must repent of our sin. And a very powerful weapon against pride is to worship God. We must come before Him with a clean heart and humble spirit. If we remain humble before Him, there will be no place for pride in our lives.

Always give God glory for all He has done in your life and for all He has given you. People should want to be around you, they should feel blessed when you speak to them. If God isn't taking first place in your life, it's time to examine yourself. Get rid of that prideful spirit and repent. We all appreciate the blessings of the Lord, but don't find yourself seeking the presents and not His presence! Worship the Creator...not the creations. It's time to get it right.

MY PRAYER: WEEK 30

Father God, thank you for being Lord of my life. You are my provider and the source of each blessing I've received. If there is anything in me that causes my ego to rise above you in my life, remove it now. I don't ever want to think that I'm better than anyone else. I don't ever want to take credit for anything that you've done in my life. Help me to be a blessing of encouragement to others and not a hindrance. I am nothing without you. All that I have is yours. Use me for your glory, in Jesus' name amen.

MY SCRIPTURES

Hebrews 3:13, Romans 13:13, Galatians 5:15,
Proverbs 13:10, Proverbs 8:13, Mark 7:21-23,
Daniel 5:20, Psalms 40:4, Galatians 6:3, Psalms 138:6

MY CHALLENGE: WEEK 30

God loves to bless His children. I'm sure there are some things that God has given you or done for you that really makes you feel good. We must always be careful to give Him the praise for all things.

This week I want you to look at all your blessings. How many of them have you truly given Him the glory for? Have you bragged on something lately? Have your words concerning your blessings lifted Him up or did they shine a light on you? How do you think others have felt after you walked away? Did they see God in your testimony, or did they feel like you achieved this thing or get this blessing on your own?

The way we represent our blessings tells others that we are either prideful or thankful to God. Let's put our ego in check this week. Give praise where praise is due. Take on humility and learn to lift up others before yourself. Pride can't survive if we don't nourish it. Focus on the feelings of others and get out of the spotlight. Let's live like Jesus.

MY PERSONAL JOURNAL

WEEK 30

MY GOALS:

MY ACCOMPLISHMENTS:

31 ~ SECRETS

Woe to those who go to great depths to hide their plans from the Lord, who think their work in darkness and think, "Who sees us? Who will know?" (Isaiah 29:15)

"Ssshhh... don't tell anyone." "No one will ever know." These are common statements used to cover up a secret. We all can see open sins of others: murder, robbery, assault, etc. But what about those sins that we can't see. You thought that lady at church was so lovable but she's really a racist. You thought that guy at school really liked you, but he went behind your back and told a lie that ruined a friendship that was very dear to you. Your best friend has been like a sister to you, but you found out recently that she has been having an affair with your husband. Secrets are silent killers. They destroy lives, relationships, and your spiritual walk with God.

The word of God teaches us in Matthew 5:21-30 that hidden sin carries the same guilt as open sin. A person who secretly hates people is just as guilty as a person who commits a hate crime openly. A person who engages in pornography behind closed doors is just as bad as the adulterer. Secret sin is something the enemy uses to trap you mentally. You not only have committed the sin, but you are hiding it. So you're actually doubling up on your sin. You should never allow yourself to think that secret sin is any less offensive than open sin.

Before you try to commit a secret act of sin, consider a few things. Man can only see what you allow him to see, but God sees your heart (1 Samuel 16:7). Nothing is done behind closed doors from God. If you think of this beforehand, maybe you'd be less inclined to take it so lightly. Hidden sin also causes you to live in hypocrisy. It's living two lives - the one that people see and one that only you (and God) can see. With hypocrisy comes guilt. The Enemy really loves to use secrets to destroy God's people.

Do you really know who you are and whose you are? As a child of God you should be an open book to the Father. There shouldn't be any pages covered up or torn out to attempt to hide from Him. Where ever you go and whatever you do, God is there. Who are you hiding from? Everything in life is not as it appears and neither are people. You may think you know your friends, family, or neighbors very well. Truth is, only God knows us completely. Don't allow secrets to take up a comfortable place in your heart.

Everything that you do in secret will be brought to light one day and you will be rewarded accordingly. If you want to do something in secret, please let it be praying to your Heavenly Father...in His secret place.

MY PRAYER: WEEK 31

Father God, I come to you today to repent from the hidden sins that I've committed. There are some things that I have done that no one knows about but you and me. Please forgive me. I don't want my secrets to cause me to turn away from you. Clean my heart from all iniquity. Remove anything that does not meet your approval. I want my words and deeds to represent Jesus Christ in my life. I want the Holy Spirit to dwell within me. I need you to help me keep my temple clean. Shine a light in all the corners of my heart so that I can see everything that must go. Secrets are no longer welcome here. Thank you for making me clean once again. I declare freedom from iniquity. No secrets... in Jesus' name, amen.

MY SCRIPTURES

Matthew 5:21-30, Romans 2:16, Ecclesiastes 12:14,
1 Corinthians 4:5, Luke 12:2-3, Proverbs 28:13,
Proverbs 23:7

MY CHALLENGE: WEEK 31

There comes a time when we have to face God with all those inner secrets. Things we haven't told anyone, but He knows. Sometimes we can carry a secret for so long it will start to eat away at our conscience.

This week, talk to God about the secrets in your life. He will not turn away from you. He wants you to bring all your cares to Him. Father God already knows every secret you are hiding. This is the time to lay that burden down, and don't pick it back up.

Maybe your secret is not something you've done. Maybe it's a thought. You need to release it to God. Don't allow the Enemy to hold you hostage through your thoughts. He can't have your soul, so he tries to grip your mind. Speak freedom right now in Jesus' name! You are no longer a prisoner of mind games. Be free!! Command victory over your life. Uncover anything that has had your mind in chains. All bondage is broken right now! Declare it and walk in total deliverance.

MY PERSONAL JOURNAL

WEEK 31

MY GOALS:

MY ACCOMPLISHMENTS:

32 ~ DEPRESSION

"Oh my soul, why be so gloomy and discouraged? Trust in God! I shall again praise Him for His wondrous help; He will make me smile again, for He is my God!" (Psalms 43:5)

When you say that someone is depressed, you suddenly think of sadness or being down in the dumps. It can last for hours, days, months, or even years if you don't get help. Some cases are considered to be medical due to something going on with a person's health or a side effect of medication. But when the problem is not temporary because of medication or health issues, depression can become a stronghold. Once it gets a grip on your emotions and mind, it will try to destroy you. In our drugged up world it is called a disease, but biblically speaking it is not. It is a mental stronghold that the enemy uses to pull you away from God.

    Let's reveal the tactics used by the Enemy to trap your mind into depression. Many times it starts with sin. You may not recognize it because it is so subtle. Ego is the tool used in this instance. The symptoms would be: feeling left out, not good enough, not appreciated, or rejected. The next symptoms: blame, anger, and isolation. The Devil is a liar and the author of confusion. Be aware of those feelings and destroy them with the word of God immediately. Once you are isolated from other children of God, the church, and the people who care for you, the Devil will come in like a flood. Your emotions take over and depression takes root. Whenever God is placed on the outside and your ego comes first, His Spirit cannot dwell within your contaminated temple and it leaves a playground for the Enemy.

    The only way to fully overcome depression is through the power of God. How? By staying in His presence. Continual prayer, studying the word, true worship, testifying of His goodness, and activating your faith. This may sound simple, but when you are depressed all this can be extremely hard to do alone. This is when you need to connect with your Christian friends, Pastor, and other church members for strength. You cannot fight this battle alone. Making yourself available for the service of God will keep your mind on Him. The word promises that He will give you perfect peace if your mind is stayed on Him! (Isaiah 26:3)

Don't take depression lightly. Consider it exactly what it is, an attack of the enemy. But this battle is the Lord's! You have the victory because you are a child of God. Be sure to stay before Him in prayer and allow the Holy Spirit to live fully in your life. Without Him you are unarmed. Protect the Spirit given to you by Father God. Keep your guard up at all times. Refuse to let your ego take the place of the Holy Spirit in your heart. You are more than a conqueror. Trust the promises of God and know that you are never alone. This storm will not overtake you.

MY PRAYER: WEEK 32

My Heavenly Father, please hear my cry for help. Depression has attacked my life and I know that it is a stronghold of the enemy. I can't fight this battle alone, but I am trusting in You to deliver me. Help me to focus on your truths and to hold on to my faith. Your word is my only hope and I put my brokenness in your hands. I declare my healing and deliverance in Jesus' name, amen.

MY SCRIPTURES

John 3:16-18, Psalms 3:4-6, Psalms 55:22, Isaiah 55:1-3, Psalms 23:4, Psalms 143:8, Psalms 119:25, Romans 15:13

MY CHALLENGE: WEEK 32

You may not be depressed at this time, but there will be times when all of us are attacked with it. The key to stopping it at the onset is identifying the Ego when it tries to rise up. When you feel your Self trying to take place of the Holy Spirit in your heart, put it in check immediately.

How to recognize it: Before making any decision to do anything, ask yourself, "Why am I doing this?" If you ask this question before making ANY decision concerning anything at all, you will control that egotistical side of yourself. Sometimes we do things because WE want to feel good, be happy, be recognized, or be something. Make your decisions according to the Spirit within. Is this what you feel God wants you to do?

Another way to stop Ego is to pray before reacting to situations. When you say things out of SELF, you can set yourself up for rejection, hurt, or many other emotional attacks. As a Christian, you must always be aware of the enemy's tricks and tactics. He is quite crafty, and your naive attitude will leave an open door for him to charge in on you. This week is all about controlling the Ego. Let your Self know that it does not take place over Holy Spirit.

If you are already in a battle with depression, now is the time to get in the word of God, stay in prayer, and find something positive to keep you busy for the Kingdom. Link up with those prayer warriors and fight your way out. His presence is your place of protection and deliverance. Run to Him like a child running to their daddy. You are much greater than the situation you are experiencing.

MY PERSONAL JOURNAL

WEEK 32

MY GOALS:

MY ACCOMPLISHMENTS:

33 ~ INTEGRITY

"I know my God, that you examine our hearts and rejoice when you find integrity there. You know I have done all this with good motives, and I have watched your people offer their gifts willingly and joyfully. Oh Lord, the God of our ancestors, Abraham, Isaac, and Israel, make your people always want to obey you. See to it that their love for You never changes." (1Chronicles 29:17-18)

Integrity is such a wonderful characteristic of a child of God. It sounds like a simple trait to have, but is it? It means to do the right thing, even if the wrong thing is so much easier; to do right even if no one is looking. It sounds like a simple request from God, but all too often we find ourselves in situations that challenge our integrity. Staying longer on a lunch break, cheating on a test, taking credit for what someone else did, allowing others to pull your weight, or taking something that was accidentally left behind by someone else are all examples of how we lose our integrity. Let's dig a little deeper.

We are living in a world where we are taught to co-exist with others. Many times we find ourselves in a gray area between good and evil just to avoid trouble. In this gray area, both sides must give up something in order for both sides to live in peace. We don't want to cause tension so we go where there is less resistance. But is that how God expects us to live?

When we're faced with choices we do one of two things: compromise or commit. Your level of integrity defines your character. Compromise can be very dangerous. You bend the rules to satisfy others, but God is not pleased. There is no gray area with God, there is only good and evil. In His Kingdom there is no such thing as compromise. You're either committed or you're not. Integrity is very valuable in the Kingdom. God knows you from the inside out and He requires all of you. That's part of the covenant you made when you accepted Jesus Christ as your Lord and Savior: you gave your all to Him. That includes living a life of integrity.

In order to be all that God wants you to be, you need to be aware of the choices you make whether someone is looking or not. When living according to His word becomes challenging, we need to ask God to give us the strength to stay committed. God promises a life of blessings if we remain pure in our integrity. Don't compromise the word of God for anything. People will remember you for what you stood up for, and laugh at what you fell for. You represent the Kingdom of God. Every decision you make should reflect His word. It doesn't matter who sees you, what does matter is what's in your heart. Only God can see that.

MY PRAYER: WEEK 33

Father God, thank you for giving me a clean heart. My desire is to walk upright before you with integrity. Help me to make good choices whether anyone can see me or not. Jesus was the perfect example for my life. I may struggle sometimes to be what you expect of me, but I know that I can do the right things and make sound decisions by following the Holy Spirit which dwells within me. Give me a desire to continue to live according to your word. Make me an example of what you expect from a child of God. In Jesus' name I pray, amen.

MY SCRIPTURES

Proverbs 12:22, 1 Timothy 5:14, Genesis 18:19, Proverbs 11:1, Proverbs 21:3, Acts 24:16, Philippians 4:8

MY CHALLENGE: WEEK 33

Living a life of integrity is pleasing to God. There are times when small things slip by unnoticed and we make poor choices that don't show very good examples of the type of life God requires of us. Sometimes they may not be little slip-ups, we intentionally do little things that seem harmless. Do we forget that we are children of God?

This week, let's take opportunities to be more careful of these stumbling blocks. Ask yourself, "What can I do to increase the integrity of my life?"

- Are you keeping your word to others, or breaking promises?
- Are you cheating someone out of something?
- Are you taking shortcuts on a job that requires more attention?
- Are you fully committed or compromising?

We can all use some improvement on how we represent God in our daily lives. Let's try to work on pleasing Him even more than ever before.

MY PERSONAL JOURNAL

WEEK 33

MY GOALS:

MY ACCOMPLISHMENTS:

34 ~ RESPECT

"Love one another warmly as Christians, and be eager to show respect for one another." (Romans 12:10)

Respect is something we all want from others. It should be something we give as well. The scripture for today not only says we should show respect, but we should be *eager* to show respect! First of all, what does respect consist of? It is basically holding in high regard. Lifting others up comes easy when it's someone we don't see often. We respect our pastor, our teachers, military officers, government officials, etc. What about the people we see every day?

Respecting others doesn't limit us to respecting people in authority. We should respect one another period. One of the main causes of people quitting their jobs is lack of respect from managers. One primary cause of arguments in the household is lack of respect for another family member. We respect people we don't see often, but disrespect the ones in our daily lives. Why is that? It's because we see all the faults in people we spend the most time with. Their faults tend to magnify because we are so quick to judge. In actuality, there is no reason to be rude or abrasive to another human being, especially if you are a child of God. If you want to gain respect from others then you should be willing to show respect. Your harshness will only stir up anger and strife.

The word of God teaches is to respect everyone in 1 Peter 2:17, wives in 1 Peter 3:7, husbands in Ephesians 5:33, parents in Exodus 20:12, governing authorities in 1 Peter 2:13-14, managers in 1 Peter 2:18, our Christian leaders in 1 Thessalonians 5:12-13, and those seeking God in 1 Peter 3:15-16. Respect is something God takes seriously. It is very important in every relationship.

Many people are living by the old motto "respect is earned." This is not scriptural and if you are a child of God you shouldn't even consider living under that motto. We don't earn respect just as we don't earn salvation. It should be freely given from our hearts as Christians. It's not always easy to respect some people, but pray and ask God to give you strength in that area. This world owes you nothing, but as a child of the King you owe Him everything. Living according to His word is your guideline. You'll be rewarded for your obedience.

Whenever you find it hard to show respect for someone, remind yourself of the grace that God has given you every day. You aren't always a saint. Your ways aren't always pleasing in His eyes, but He still shows mercy on you. His love is unconditional. Do you actually deserve God's perfect love? Can you show a little more respect and compassion to others knowing that you aren't "all that" yourself?

MY PRAYER: WEEK 34

Dear Heavenly Father, thank you for loving me even when I'm not so lovable. I haven't always loved or respected others as much as I know I should. Forgive me for it today. Help me to be more respectful not only to the people in authority but to my household, family members, and friends. I realize that I am not even deserving of your unconditional love and grace. Thank you for granting me so many blessings that I really don't deserve. Help me to see people through your eyes and not through my own. In Jesus' name I pray, amen.

MY SCRIPTURES

1 Peter 2:17, 1 Peter 3:7, Ephesians 5:33, Exodus 20:12,
1 Peter 2:13-14, 1 Peter 2:18,
1 Thessalonians 5:12-13

MY CHALLENGE: WEEK 3

Respecting others is something most of us were taught from childhood. You may think that this is just a subject that doesn't pertain to you, but we all can use a little brushing up on the respect level in our lives.

This week look at opportunities you have to show respect to others that you don't normally consider. Open a door for a person in front of you, tell a family member how much you appreciate them, back down from an argument and consider the fact that it's not gaining anything. Give honor where you would normally just walk away. This is very pleasing to the Father.

While giving out respect, also learn to respect yourself. Don't make drastic decisions just to be accepted by others. Set boundaries and don't allow anyone to drag you outside of them. Respecting yourself enough to stand firm on God's word is the best respect you can give yourself. Respect, just like love, is an action word. Put it into action in your life and allow it to flow into the lives of the ones around you.

MY PERSONAL JOURNAL

WEEK 34

MY GOALS:

MY ACCOMPLISHMENTS:

35 ~ WHAT MY FRUIT LOOKS LIKE

"But the fruit of the Spirit is love, joy, peace, patience, kindness, goodness, faithfulness, gentleness, and self-control. Against such things there is no law. Those who belong to Christ Jesus have crucified the sinful nature with its passions and desires. Since we live by the Spirit, let us keep in step with the Spirit." (Galatians 5:22-25)

Have you ever known a person who says they are a child of God yet they are always grumpy? How about the Christian who always has something bad or negative to talk about. I'm not saying they aren't saved. Salvation comes from God, not me. But as Christians, we should allow our character to grow and mature so that we become more Christ-like. The inner transformation should show in our character and therefore the fruits of the Spirit should be evident in our lives.

Building and developing our character to does not come overnight. One sermon won't do it. It doesn't sneak up from behind and take over you. It comes from the Holy Spirit. By living in Spiritual discipline, obedience, and faith, the fruits of the Spirit will begin to manifest in your life. When you truly love Jesus, stay in God's presence, and apply the word to your life daily these fruits will become your very being. Commit yourself to having the fruits of the Spirit active in your life.

Love: It desires to seek and apply what God has to say in your life.

Joy: It will cause you to enjoy your relationship with Christ.

Peace: It will allow you to control your tone and keep your composure in difficult situations

Patience: It shows tolerance.

Kindness: Is Jesus' love becoming tangible through you towards others.

Goodness: To do good and be good. God's own nature.
Faithfulness: Is the glue that keeps you there when it's easier to walk away.
Gentleness: It shows calmness in someone else's storm.
Self-Control: Is allowing God to be in control when you want to blow up.

The fruits of the Spirit are for our betterment and for God's glory. Once we are filled with the Holy Spirit, they should begin to grow. Don't take them for granted for they are very costly. Jesus paid for these fruits on Calvary. Many people don't carry these fruits because they aren't willing to sacrifice their selfish desires. You should consider it an honor that God would choose you to bear fruit. Show your appreciation today by letting your fruit blossom into healthy, good fruit. These are the very characteristics of Christ, and they should be yours as well.

MY PRAYER: WEEK 35

Dear Heavenly Father, thank you for the fruits of the Spirit that Jesus paid for on Calvary. My desire is to have the character of Jesus in my life every day. Help me to develop my character to be pleasing to you. I declare that my life will be fruitful and beautiful in your eyes. As I allow the Holy Spirit to transform me from the inside out, help me to walk in obedience and discipline to you will. Teach me through your word. In Jesus' name, amen.

MY SCRIPTURES

Galatians 5:22-25

As you begin to grow in Christ, your fruits will grow as well. This week you will ask yourself a few questions in regards to each fruit. This will allow you to pay closer attention to your spiritual "fruit tree".

> **Love:** Are you motivated to do for others, or are you expecting something in return?
> **Joy:** Are you experiencing true joy, or is your happiness dependent on others?
> **Peace:** Are you living in the peace that passes all understanding (Philippians 4:6-7) or are you shattered at the very sight of storms in your life?
> **Patience:** Are you able to keep a Godly perspective in the face of adversity, or are you easily ticked off?
> **Kindness:** Are you serving others from your heart or tending to your own needs and desires first?
> **Goodness:** Does your life reflect the holiness of God and His character? Do you desire to see others in a deep relationship with God?
> **Faithfulness:** Are you dependable to Jesus as well as to others?
> **Gentleness:** Do you come across as arrogant, brash, or headstrong? Are you allowing the Holy Spirit to flow through you naturally?
> **Self-Control:** Is your ego and fleshly desires controlling your life or are you allowing the Spirit to guide you to do what pleases God and serves others?

Whenever you aren't walking by the Spirit, He will convict you, causing you to feel a spiritual guilt when you are not walking in step to the Spirit. Whenever you miss the mark, you can always ask God's forgiveness. He will empower you through the Holy Spirit to walk in His way. Your fruit is so beautiful in the Father's eyes. Continue to grow. Your fruit has such a holy aroma in the Kingdom!

MY PERSONAL JOURNAL

WEEK: 35

MY GOALS:

MY ACCOMPLISHMENTS:

36 ~ PATIENCE

"My brethren count it all joy when you fall into various trials, knowing this, that the testing of your faith works patience. But let patience have her perfect work, that you may be perfect and entire, lacking nothing." (James 1:2-4)

I don't know anyone who welcomes trials and tribulations with joy. Really, let's be honest here. Who says, "Oh boy, another chance to show patience...hooray!" As much as we love things to run smoothly every day, we all know that at some point there will be interruptions that will test our faith. It reminds me of the competition game shows when you think everything is in your favor, until the host throws a wrench in the mix. That's when your true skills are tested.

We probably don't consider the word "faith" when we talk about patience. Patience is actually the evidence of your inner strength. Impatient people are spiritually weak, meaning they don't have the inner strength that Paul prayed for in Colossians 1:11. The key to obtaining this inner strength is having faith in the power of God. It's through this faith that God channels patience into you. Patience is one of the fruits of the Spirit, but the Holy Spirit empowers through *"hearing with faith"* according to Galatians 3:5. So in all honesty, if you have a problem with patience, you need to build up your faith.

Now let's get to the core of patience. Another definition would be longsuffering or slow to anger. 1 Corinthians 13:4 says, *"love is patient and kind"*. Those five words alone should tell you it won't be easy. We must love the unlovable and be kind to them! This will definitely require patience...and faith. When you experience love there will come a time when your heart will be broken, your faith tested, and your patience put on display. Not just in close relationships, but love in any form will eventually require pure patience. As a child of God, you are commanded to love. There is no other option. So in order to love like Jesus teaches, you must perfect your patience and faith. It's going to take Jesus to make you love some people. It's going to take His power for you to have patience with them too.

How can you build your inner strength or patience level? Much prayer will be required. Once you ask God for more patience, prepare yourself to be tested to your limits. It's not going to be a walk in the park. Just imagine how many people approached Jesus with what we would consider "dumb questions". Imagine how many times He must have just stood there and smiled. He is our role model. We certainly will have moments when we want to grit our teeth. That's fine. Grit if you must. Just know that you are being perfected for the glory of God. Count it all joy!

<u>MY PRAYER: WEEK 36</u>

Father God, I thank you for your perfect love. Thank you for having patience with me. Help me to see others through your eyes and not my own. My heart's desire is to be all that you created me to be. Open my heart to receive your love completely so that I can in turn give complete love to others. As I allow your love to flow through me, allow my faith to become even stronger. As my faith increases, allow divine patience to become a virtue in my life. I know that in order for my patience to grow, I will be tested. Let the power of the Holy Spirit rise up in me like never before. Make me more like Jesus. Transform my mind and my heart, in Jesus' name, amen.

HIS PEARL I AM...a work in progress

MY SCRIPTURES

Luke 23:34, Romans 2:4, Hebrews 6:9-15, Psalms 37:7, Proverbs 16:32, 2 Peter 1:5-7

MY CHALLENGE: WEEK 36

Is your patience being tested? Just consider it as boot camp, you are being trained for Godliness. As you go through these tests, it is very important to stay focused on the Lord.

This week take a look at your tests before responding. Extinguish the flames before they blow up. When you find yourself murmuring under your breath, take time to look up to God for strength. Walk away from a person who causes you to get upset, pray, and then approach them with love and kindness.

Patience takes a whole lot of practice. You definitely won't master it in a week. Make it a point to work on this virtue regularly. Look at people through the eyes of Jesus. Remember that *"God's kindness led you toward repentance"* (Romans 2:4) So the kindness of God through you may lead others to repentance too. I really believe this is why God wants us to perfect our patience. It's all about the Kingdom of God.

If you look at your Spiritual growth as an opportunity for others to gain salvation, then you will find more strength and motivation to endure the tests of faith and patience. You can do this!

MY PERSONAL JOURNAL

WEEK 36

MY GOALS:

MY ACCOMPLISHMENTS:

37 ~ TEMPER, TEMPER

"My dear brothers and sisters, take note of this: Everyone should be quick to listen, slow to speak and slow to become angry. Those who consider themselves religious and yet do not keep a tight rein on their tongues deceive themselves, and their religion is worthless." (James 1:19, 26)

If we could record ourselves each time we flew off the handle at someone, we might actually see how arguments could have been avoided. Some people are very easily provoked and others have to be careful about what they say and how they say it to prevent a fight from starting. As Christians we should be willing and able to tame our tongues. If you truly have the love of God working within your heart, it shouldn't be that complicated.

    Let's dissect the bad temper for a moment. Your temper is contagious. All it takes is for one person to start yelling and before you know it everyone involved is yelling. Do you know where the root of a bad temper is created? It's created in "Self". The need to be right. You can't lose your temper if you have Self under control. Another element of a bad temper is "Pride". When you feel like your opinion is worth more than anyone else's and you refuse to think otherwise, then your temper will flare up when your opinion is challenged. The third element is "Envy". When your "Self" feelings are hurt or you are envious of another person and you feel like they are superior in any way, you will experience an inner rage. You may be too proud to show your "Envy", but it will cause your temper to eat away at you from the inside. When you love yourself more than others, you tend to care less about their feelings. Therefore, you're quick to get angry and lose your temper.

Now that you know where your bad temper originates, how do you control it? By knowing who you are in Christ. When you truly realize how powerful God's divine love for you really is, then you will be more willing to subdue that temper and show more love and consideration towards others. You must be willing to allow the love of God to manifest in your life every day. Before losing your temper, step back and see what the root of the problem is. Control your "Self" and your tongue. Words are so dangerous. Once they are released, you can never erase the pain they will cause. You cannot and will not win every disagreement. It's ok to just let it go and let God take over.

Take a long look at your own life. I'm sure you can find things that you've done or said that God should be very angry with you about...but He didn't strike you with lightening and throw things at you. Control that tongue of yours. Your words should be bearing fruits of the Spirit, not cursing another's soul. Get a grip! It's going to be alright.

MY PRAYER: WEEK 37

Dear Heavenly Father, thank you for not losing your temper with me when I did things against your teaching. I have sometimes lost my temper with others without even thinking of their feelings. I actually intended to hurt their feelings out of my own personal rage. Lord, open my heart so that I can allow your perfect love to flow through me. Help me to control my temper by controlling my "Self". Forgive me for not always having it together. Forgive me for the things I've done and said to hurt others. I am so much better than that. Today I claim power over my Self, my tongue, and my temper in Jesus' name, amen.

MY SCRIPTURES

Proverbs 19:11, Psalms 35:28, Psalms 37:30, Proverbs 15:2, Proverbs 21:23, Ephesians 4:26-32, Romans 12:21, John 8:7, 1 Peter 3:8-11,

MY CHALLENGE: WEEK 37

Everyone doesn't have a quick temper, but we all have moments when we speak before we think. Working on thinking before we speak is something that we all can do.

This week I want you to pray for God to show you how you can work on controlling your "Self" and consider the feelings of others more. You should always remember that in every situation, you are representing Christ - even in moments of anger. How you handle yourself can be a great tool to winning others to Him.

You are a child of God and you are also human. There will be times that you just can't hold your peace. Repent and ask the people you offended to forgive you. Standing for peace and Godliness is what matters. Be an example of how powerful the love of God can be if you surrender to Him completely. Ephesians 4:26 says "anger and sin not". The sin is not in being angry, it's in how you act or what you do when you're angry. The power is in your hands through the Holy Spirit. Use that power wisely!

MY PERSONAL JOURNAL

WEEK 37

MY GOALS:

MY ACCOMPLISHMENTS:

38 ~ THE POWER OF LUST

"Dear friends, I urge you, as foreigners and exiles, to abstain from sinful desires, which wage war against your soul." (1 Peter 2:11)

Every day of our lives, we make choices. Some small and some great, but still we make them. There is an old saying that says, "Not to decide is to decide already." In other words, if you need to make a choice and don't choose to say "no" openly, then you're saying "yes" in your heart.

Lust is having a deep desire for something that you cannot, or should not have. The power that lust can have over you is not in the one-time choice to do wrong, it's in the choice to continue to do it. Lust has a rebound effect that the enemy doesn't want you to be aware of. You get close to something you know you shouldn't be dabbling with, you step away from it and then you go back to it even closer than you were the first time. After awhile, you find yourself in the grips of lust. If you would have made the open choice not to go there in the first place, you wouldn't have fallen into the trap. By not making that choice, you were saying "yes" to it.

Old habits, thoughts, and behaviors will lead you directly into the hands of the very thing you need to avoid. As a child of God, you have the power through the Holy Spirit to renew your mind. You need to be aware of your weaknesses and stay away from situations that will cause you to get caught up. You already know what you can and cannot handle, and so does the enemy. You also know that the tactics of the devil are unfair. He will use your weakness to bring you down every time. Why would you open yourself up to something so obvious? Use your God-given discernment to see trouble coming your way. If you devote more time to God in service, worship, and prayer and less time to focusing on things that will bring you into the pit of lust, then you'd be able to withstand the battle and overcome.

The word of God teaches us in Titus 2:11-12 that God's grace can and will offer guidance for us in these situations. Paul even admitted that he had prayed three times for God to deliver him from an unspoken matter. That's when God said, *"My grace is sufficient for you, my power is made perfect in weakness." (2 Corinthians 12:9)*. Sometimes we hunger greatly for something that looks good to us, but it's not good for us. If you fail to take heed of the warnings, these desires will lead to death in your spiritual life. The wages of sin is death, (Romans 6:23). Remember this, the word of God tells you how you will be rewarded before you decide to do something for Him. The Enemy never shows the outcome, he just shows you the temporary pleasure of your sin. Why would you allow yourself to be tricked into something for selfish, temporary pleasure when God promises an eternity of life with Him? Think about it before you say "yes" to sin again.

MY PRAYER: WEEK 38

Father God, thank you for giving me discernment to know when I may be heading for trouble. Forgive me for not always saying "no" to my lustful desires. Renew your Spirit in me, transform my mind, and give me the willpower to say "yes" to your will. Deliver me from this weakness. Through your love, mercy, and grace I know that I am a conqueror. Don't take your Spirit away from me, but allow me to walk according to your word. Use me to help others overcome their weaknesses. Empower me through your word in Jesus' name, amen.

MY SCRIPTURES

Ephesians 4:21-23, Matthew 7:13, Colossians 3:5-6,
1 Corinthians 13:4-8

MY CHALLENGE: WEEK 38

Lust is something that the church doesn't discuss too often. I say, "If the word talks about it, we should talk about it too."

Lust is a sin that can lead to terrible actions like: pornography, rape, incest, sexual addictions, child abuse, and even murder. This is a demonic force and entertaining it just a little can cause traumatic results. Statistics say 1 in 5 girls and 1 in 20 boys is a victim of childhood sexual abuse. 20% of adult females and 5-10% of adult males recall a childhood sexual assault act from their childhood. 3 out of 4 of these acts were done by a friend or family member. (Source: www.victimsofcrime.org)

Learning the difference between love and lust is an important lesson to teach and learn. 1 Corinthians 13:4-8 tells us what love is. **Lust is the very opposite.** Lust is: not kind, envies, behaves rudely, seeks for its own pleasures, thinks evil, rejoices in sin, perverts the truth, seeks self gratification, fails to achieve lasting satisfaction, cares only for itself, and will hurt, destroy, deceive, and lie.

This week search your heart and ask God to remove any lustful desires that you may be struggling with. If you or someone you know are, or have been, a victim of sexual abuse get help immediately. **For more information go to: https://www.rainn.org/get-help, or call: 1-800-656-HOPE.**

God loves you and He wants you to be whole, healed, and delivered! Turn to Him today.

MY PERSONAL JOURNAL

WEEK 38

MY GOALS:

MY ACCOMPLISHMENTS:

39 ~ GREED

Then he said to them, "Beware, and be on your guard against every form of greed; for not even when one has an abundance does his life consist of his possessions." (Luke 12:15)

As responsible adults, we should always prepare for the future. There is no harm in it. It's actually wise to be ready for certain economic times in your life. We also know that leaving an inheritance for your children is a biblical teaching (Proverbs 13:22). But what happens when you become obsessed with having more?

Greed is defined as having an intense desire for something, especially wealth or power. In today's scripture Jesus warns us by saying *"Beware"*. We are warned against the snare of greed and putting our confidence in our possessions. Your life should not be defined by what you own. If you are focused more on your earthly possessions than you are on your relationship with God, then you have a serious problem. As a child of God, you should know that He will supply all your needs, He wants you to prosper, and you were created for His glory. If you've truly accepted Jesus into your life, material possessions would not be your main concern. Ask yourself, "What am I really hungering for?"

Did you know that God always rewards those who put Him first in all things? Matthew 6:31-33 teaches us that if we seek the Kingdom of God and all His righteousness, everything else that we need will be given to us. The key is prioritizing. Keeping Him first. How do you do that? By seeking Him before making decisions, by offering up your first fruits (tithes) to Him, by building a strong relationship with Him, by allowing Him to really be the head of your entire life.

Jesus taught all throughout His ministry that there are three things of supreme importance to God: Loving Him with all our heart, loving one another, and seeking after God's Kingdom. If you dedicate your life to doing these three things, everything else will fall into place. When you become greedy for your own selfish desire, you lose focus on what really matters to God. When you aren't doing what matters to Him, then you lose out. Have you ever seen how some millionaires go crazy if they can't continue to make more money? When the stock markets crash, people commit suicide because they can't handle losing their money and possessions. God loves to see you prosper, when He gets the glory for it. He wants you to be an example to others of how well He provides for those who seek Him first. Get your priorities in order. Watch how much easier it is when you do it God's way. Leave your family a legacy of trusting God and keeping Him first. Eternal blessings await!

MY PRAYER: WEEK 39

Dear Heavenly Father, thank you so much for being the supplier of all my needs. You are my source and my provider. I put all my trust in only You. Forgive me for the times I may have put my heart into my possessions or gaining more money instead of on your Kingdom. There is nothing I desire more than You. Help me to keep my priorities in order. In Jesus' name I pray, amen.

MY SCRIPTURES

Matthew 6:31-33, Luke 12:13-21, Proverbs 15:27, Proverbs 28:22, Mark 8:36, Psalms 50:10

MY CHALLENGE: WEEK 39

Greed is something that can affect everyone. It doesn't always pertain to money or riches. Let's examine ourselves this week for the spirit of greed that may be in other areas of our lives.

Take inventory of all the things that mean a lot to you. Do you focus on any of those things more than you focus on studying God's word? Do you value them more than your prayer time? How about food? Do you tend to be "greedy" when you eat? Why are you continuing to stuff your stomach if you know you're full? Are you hogging the limelight from others when you are the center of attention? Why not share the light with others. Give honor where it is due. When you see something on sale, do you buy as much as you can? Why? Are you giving some of it away to be a blessing to others or are you cramming your cupboards?

Greed can ring the doorbell to each and every one of us. It's up to us to put it in check. Don't ever allow it to come between you and the Kingdom of God. He can and will supply all your needs according to His riches in glory (Philippians 4:19). Will you trust Him to do it?

MY PERSONAL JOURNAL

WEEK 39

MY GOALS:

MY ACCOMPLISHMENTS:

40 ~ JEALOUSY

"Anger is cruel and fury overwhelming, but who can stand before jealousy?"
(Proverbs 27:4)

There's an old saying, "They're trying to keep up with the Joneses." Whatever happened to the days when people would be happy for the success of others? If you really think about it...those days never existed! There is always someone, somewhere wishing they had what another person has. Jealousy is worse than anger in the eyes of God. It's like you saying, "God must love them more than me. What He gave me is not good enough. I deserve better than this." If you are a child of God, then you must believe His word. Psalms 84:11 says *"...no good thing does He withhold from those who walk blameless before Him."*

Before you find yourself falling into the trap of jealousy, identify the root of why you may feel that way. There are three things that may cause jealousy to slip into your heart. First there is insecurity. When you desire something that someone else has, you speak negativity into your heart. You feel as if you don't deserve the same thing, you're not good enough, or you don't measure up to others standards. This is where insecurities take root. Secondly, you have placed unrealistic expectations on yourself. This causes you to feel as if things don't come to you quick enough and your impatience causes you to be jealous when you see someone else with something you've been working so hard to get. Finally, there is your sense of entitlement. You feel as if you deserve that "thing" more than the person who has it.

You must remember this, don't be jealous of what someone else has. God may have withheld it from you because it will cause you pain and heartache later. You may not have it because you cannot handle what you have to go through to get it. And then, you may not have it because God has something better for you. The main thing you should do is be thankful for what you already have! God doesn't love you any less than anyone else. We all have certain promises lined up especially for us, if we stay in the will of God. Keep your mind focused on the Kingdom and you will be rewarded accordingly. Trust the Lord and keep His desires first in your life. The blessings He has in store for you are much greater than anything you could ask or even think of for yourself. Celebrate the blessings of others. Don't let jealousy kill your dreams.

In order to defeat jealousy you must be willing to change the way you think (Romans 12:2), take your thoughts captive (2 Corinthians 10:5), and have the mind of Christ (Philippians 2:2-4). Let the word of God take root in your heart. Love like Jesus commanded. Only a pure love can overcome a jealous spirit. Get your love level up!

MY PRAYER: WEEK 40

Gracious, Heavenly Father, thank you for blessing me so much. Thank you for being my provider and giving me what I don't deserve. Forgive me for ever feeling that I deserve what belongs to someone else. Give me a loving heart, a heart like Jesus so that I may love more and covet less. I don't want to make you feel like I am ungrateful. Help me to stay in my lane and appreciate what you've already given me. I realize that by desiring what someone else has, I am blocking what you have in store for me. Clean my heart so that I may be open for what you have for me. I will give you the glory and all honor. In Jesus' name I pray, amen.

MY SCRIPTURES

Psalms 84:11, 1 Corinthians 3:1-3, 13:4-5, James 4:1-2, Ecclesiastes 4:4Proverbs 14:30, Ezekiel 16:42, Exodus 20:17

MY CHALLENGE: WEEK 40

Jealousy is something that no one wants to admit is in their heart. You may not even realize that it's in your heart because it can be so subtle. Whether it's a big problem for you, or you may not see it as being an issue, jealousy can grow quickly into a monster if left unchecked.

This week we are shining the light into the corners of our hearts to expose that ugly spirit. Is there something you saw someone else with that just made your heart leap with desire? Ladies, this may be a pair of shoes, a new purse, an engagement ring, or any other item that caused you to want for yourself. Men, this may be a car, some sporting equipment, a woman, or any other thing that just caused you to desire more than what you already have. Jealousy isn't always over material things. Maybe you are jealous of another person's ministry, job, or lifestyle. Beware: You don't know what they had to go through to get it!

Let's focus on our own relationship with God and trust Him to bless us with the things He can trust us with. There's an old saying, "if you want to make God laugh, tell Him about your dreams." My friend, God has more in store for you than you could ever imagine. All you need to do is stay in His will and trust that His promises to you will never be broken. If you do what you're supposed to do, He will do what He has promised.

MY PERSONAL JOURNAL

WEEK 40

MY GOALS:

MY ACCOMPLISHMENTS:

41 ~ THE TONGUE

"A good man brings good things out of the good stored up in his heart, and an evil man brings evil out of the evil stored up in his heart. For the mouth speaks what the heart is full of." (Luke 6:45)

Words are very powerful. They can build you up or tear you down. They can comfort you or kill you. It's totally up to you to decide how you use them. If you are a child of God, you should be using them to encourage and inspire others. You should also be using them to speak life into the lives of this hopeless generation. That little muscle in your mouth can be the most powerful weapon in your arsenal. Where does it get its strength? It develops all of its power directly from your heart!

Your heart determines the control of sin in your life. Sin develops in your heart, then moves to your head, then is manifested by using your body parts. The tongue is the sharpest part of your body. Words cut deep into the hearts of others when used by the enemy. You can never even think of taming your tongue until you learn to tame your heart. Your relationship with God will determine whether your heart is tame or not.

If you are speaking negativity, then you will live in negativity. If you are speaking failure, stupidity, worthlessness, and hopelessness over your children then that's what will manifest. As children of God, we are to speak life and power into the lives of everyone we come in contact with. The only way you can do that is to have that belief in your heart. Why on earth would a Christian use words to tear down others? They do it because they have not completely allowed the love of God into their lives. They believe IN God and accept Jesus as Savior, but they don't allow the power OF God to change their hearts.

Living with hatred and negativity in your heart will keep the Holy Spirit from working in your life. Your words will either activate or deactivate the power of God. In order to tame your tongue, you must first give your heart to Jesus. Not just lip service but heart service. Accepting Christ into your life is a lot more than a verbal acceptance. If you haven't allowed Him into your heart, then your tongue will control your life.

God calls us to cultivate a habit of speaking life. A cultivated heart will produce a tamed tongue, which will in turn produce words of love, life, mercy, grace, and encouragement. Is your heart totally turned over to God? If not, this is the time to get it right. When you don't know how to fix something, you go to the manufacturer's book called the "Owner's Manual". If you want your heart fixed, go to the word of God. Once that heart is fixed, the words coming from your mouth will be guided by the Holy Spirit. Speak Life!

MY PRAYER: WEEK 41

Father God, thank you for opening my mind to this teaching about the power of my tongue. I may not have realized that my words are generated from my heart. Forgive me for using words to condemn, hurt, or create negativity in the lives of others. Clean my heart so that the Holy Spirit can work and speak through me. I want to speak life into my family, friends, and loved ones. I want my words to change the lives of others. Help me to control the words coming out of my mouth. Make me aware of the times that my heart isn't right with you. I declare today that I will do whatever it takes to keep my heart clean so that my words are speaking your will into the lives of others and over my own life. In Jesus' name, amen.

MY SCRIPTURES

Proverbs 18:21, James Chapter 3, Proverbs 17:27, Leviticus 19:16, 1 Peter 3:10, Matthew 12:36-37, Ephesians 4:29, Psalms 141:3

MY CHALLENGE: WEEK 41

Speaking comes from your heart. We must be very careful of the feelings we hold within our hearts. If someone has done or said something to offend you, pray about it before confronting them. Speaking out of anger will cause you to say some things that you'll regret. Once words are released from your mouth, the damage has already been done. No matter how much you apologize, that person will always remember what you said to them.

This week let's learn to bridle our tongues. We must think before we speak. If you find yourself filled with emotions, this is the perfect time to hold off before saying anything. Follow this check list before spouting off:

- Do I really need to say this?
- What is my real motive for saying this?
- Will these words hurt or help someone?
- Will these words draw me closer to God, or cause me to be further from Him?
- Will these words cause division between me and the person I'm speaking to?

Spend some time in prayer about the things you've been holding in your heart. Until you deal with those inner feelings, your heart will be a breeding ground for damaging words. Bring it all to God.

MY PERSONAL JOURNAL

WEEK 41

MY GOALS:

MY ACCOMPLISHMENTS:

42 ~ SPIRITUAL DANGER

"If I have the gift of prophecy and can fathom all mysteries and all knowledge, and if I have a faith that can move mountains, but I do not have love, I am nothing." (1 Corinthians 13:2)

If you truly love God, you should want to spend time with Him every day. Learning more about Him through His word should be your deepest desire. Did you know that there can also be potential danger in knowing too much about Him? Sounds absurd doesn't it?

Seeking God on a regular basis is very rewarding. When we get closer to Him, we gain more and more knowledge about Him. So, how can this actually be very dangerous? Knowledge can corrupt and distract you if you don't know what to do with it! 1 Corinthians 8:1 says, *"Knowledge puffs up, but love builds up."* The scripture today tells us that we can have all knowledge, but if we don't have love to go with it, then we have nothing. How can this happen? It can happen when we get so deep into studying the word that we think we're "above" others. We get so "heavenly bound until we're no earthly good." In other words, when you consider yourself a scholar of the word, but have no love or compassion for the lost souls out there, then you are not pleasing God.

Knowing the bible from cover to cover but not applying the principles to your life can destroy your soul. Loving God and knowing about Him are two different things. You are responsible for everything you know about God and His word. It's your job to teach others, not hoard all of it for yourself. Teach others how to get into His presence, how to worship, and how to pray. That is your responsibility. Your knowledge of God is to be used to change the lives of others.

By all means, we should get to know everything we can about our Father. In getting that knowledge we must also get an understanding of what to do with it (Proverbs 4:7). In order to balance out the knowledge you acquire, you must learn to do three things. Stay amazed, don't become complacent. God gives new mercies every day, don't take them for granted. Tell Him how awesome He is each day. Secondly, stay dependent on God. Keep an active prayer life, communicating with Him is good for your soul. It keeps you grounded and humble. Finally, always focus on Jesus. Love Him with all your being and pattern your life after His. If you do this you leave no room for a haughty spirit.

You were called to be a disciple, not a ruler. Use all your knowledge to benefit the Kingdom. Your greater anointing comes at a great price. Never consider yourself to be greater than anyone. We are all children of God. Your goal should be training up other brothers and sisters in Christ.

MY PRAYER: WEEK 42

Father God, thank you so much for your word. The more I know about you, the more I love you. I don't ever want to get complacent, taking you for granted. I don't ever want to think I'm better than anyone else because I study your word and have a desire to know even more. Lord, help me use the knowledge of you and your word to be a blessing to others. Open my heart not only to receive from you, but to give to others the wisdom and knowledge planted inside of me. I rebuke any haughty or puffed up spirit that tries to dwell in my heart. The only danger I want is to be a danger to the Enemy's camp. I give you all honor, all glory, and all praise! Use me for your purpose in Jesus' name, amen.

MY SCRIPTURES

Psalms 19:7-9, Proverbs 4:7, Luke 12:48,
2 Peter 3:18, Colossians 3:16

MY CHALLENGE: WEEK 42

When you love the Lord with all your heart, you can't help but want to stay in His presence and know Him even more. There is nothing at all wrong with that. The thing we must remember is, there is a lost and dying world out there who needs to know Him too.

This week let's share what we know about Father God with someone else. Whether it's a special experience you've had with Him, a powerful scripture, or even a new revelation on a scripture you've been studying. Your purpose as a disciple of Jesus Christ is to share His love with the world. Focus on ways that you can use what you know about God to bless someone. Let your love for the Father shine from your heart. What good is all your knowledge of Him going to do if you don't have love?

MY PERSONAL JOURNAL

WEEK 42

MY GOALS:

MY ACCOMPLISHMENTS:

43 ~ HOMELESS

"Therefore we do not lose heart. Though outwardly we are wasting away, yet inwardly we are being renewed day by day. For our light and momentary troubles are achieving for us an eternal glory that far outweighs them all. So we fix our eyes not on what is seen, but on what is unseen. For what is seen is temporary, but what is unseen is eternal." (2 Corinthians 4:16-18)

I want to dedicate this devotion to my dear friends, Ashley and Carlos Robinson. They have headed up a wonderful ministry (Divine Intervention Ministry) helping the homeless, needy, and lost. When I think of all the people this ministry alone has touched, I just want to praise God.

Have you ever wondered what it must be like to be homeless and how frustrating it could be? Every one of us have had dreams, goals, and plans of a successful life. I'm sure being homeless was never on the list. I read an article one time that stated many Americans are only one paycheck away from being homeless. These people never planned to be where they are. Sometimes a series of unfortunate events can take you for a whirlwind and land you in the pits of emptiness. It can happen to anyone.

So what exactly is homelessness? The dictionary says that it's the state of not having a permanent residence. That's how society sees homelessness. But God's standards are different than man's. If a homeless man or woman has accepted Jesus as their Lord and Savior, then they are not homeless anymore! You see, the definition "not having permanent residence" would be describing the people who don't know Jesus. I wonder how many sinners have driven past a homeless person and said, "that poor homeless man..." not even realizing that if that homeless man has received Christ, and they have not...then they are the one who's homeless! That sinner's homelessness is more permanent than that homeless man's.

Homelessness on this earth is temporary. God can change those situations around by using ministries like Ashley and Carlos Robinson's Divine Intervention Ministry. But even with all your success, fulfilled dreams, and accomplishments, if you don't know Jesus as Lord and Savior your world will come crashing down leaving you in an eternal homeless situation. None of us plan to be homeless on earth, so why would you plan to be homeless for eternity? If you haven't accepted Jesus Christ, then that's exactly what you are doing. You can't always control your surroundings or circumstances in this life, but you have all control how the end of your story is written. Chose today. When you see another homeless person you should ask yourself, "Am I homeless?"

MY PRAYER: WEEK 43

Heavenly Father, thank you for giving me an eternal home in Heaven. I have never compared homelessness on earth to eternal life, but I am so thankful that I don't have to worry about where I'll be after I leave this earthly life as long as Jesus Christ is my Lord and Savior. Help me to show others the way to Heaven. Let my life be a light in their dark places. Just the thought of not having eternity with you breaks my heart. I am so grateful for Jesus preparing a place just for me. Help me to stay on the right track so that will make it in and that I will bring many, many more with me. In Jesus name, amen.

MY SCRIPTURES

2 Corinthians 5:1-5

This scripture is so powerful and goes perfectly with this devotion. Let it take root in your spirit and meditate on it all week.

MY CHALLENGE: WEEK 43

There is so much that we take for granted every day. Food we eat, clothes, shelter, cars, and family are things we don't even thank God for anymore. For a moment each day, think of how your life would be if you were homeless. Put yourself out there in the bad weather, in the middle of those crime filled streets, watching people overdose, fighting for food, and not knowing if you'll live to see the next day.

We never want to put ourselves in that scenario, but it's a reality to so many. Your challenge this week is to find a homeless ministry to reach out to. You may not want to go out on the streets, but donate something or ask how you can help in other ways. Part two of the challenge this week is to witness to someone who has not accepted Jesus Christ as their Lord and Savior. Pray with them. Consider it like you're helping them find a new place to live. You're their real estate broker! The place is already paid for. All they have to do is accept the gift of salvation and the keys will belong to them!

MY PERSONAL JOURNAL

WEEK 43

MY GOALS:

MY ACCOMPLISHMENTS:

44 ~ WHAT DO YOU BELIEVE?

Then Jesus said, "Did I not tell you that if you believe, you will see the glory of God?" (John 11:40)

Have you ever seen the glory of God? The answer is yes, you have. If you said "no", it's only because you don't know exactly what it is. Until you know what it is you cannot believe, therefore you have not seen. The glory of God is not just physical or material, it is a beauty that emanates from His character. It is the beauty of His Spirit. It can fill the earth or adorn a person. When the glory of God is upon a person, you will often see it in their countenance. They radiate pure love and inner beauty. It's the very beauty of their Spirit. The difference in a person's glory and God's glory is that a person's glory is fallible, it eventually passes away until God allows it to be seen again. God's glory is eternal, it is the essence of who He is and the revelation of His being. Isaiah 43:7 teaches that God created us for His glory. This literally means that we glorify Him through our gifts such as music, love, heroism, etc. In 2 Corinthians 4:7 it reminds us that we are vessels that contain His glory. Nature also exhibits the glory of God in the beauty of flowers, fresh breezes, flowing water, birds singing, etc. It is through us and through nature that God is able to reveal Himself to all of humanity. We see His glory every day. So now that you know what it is, you can surely say "Yes, I've seen His glory."

Now that you know what His glory is, you must believe these five things about Him in order to experience His glory in a deeper level.

- God loves you - Romans 5:8
- God will provide for you - Philippians 4:19

- God will deliver you - Psalms 91:14-15
- God is for you - Romans 8:31
- God is with you - Hebrews 13:5

Experiencing God's glory is very overwhelming when you are worshipping Him. You'll feel His love overtake you. It's almost unbearable, but so beautiful. One of the greatest experiences as a child of God is getting into His presence in deep prayer and allowing Him to fill the room with pure glory! It's during these special moments that bondages are broken off your life, burdens are lifted, and indescribable peace comes upon you. I encourage you to seek His presence daily. Let the glory of God fall upon you. It's such a wonderful feeling to know that you can actually feel His unconditional love when you worship Him in Spirit and in truth. Make your special time with Father God the most important part of your day, every day.

MY PRAYER: WEEK 44

Father God, I come to you today just to say thank you. Thank you for allowing me to see your glory. What an awesome God you are! How amazing is your love for me! I am so humbled to see your glory in the skies, the trees, the flowers, and in all creation. My desire is to be in your presence. Let your glory fill my room as I pray. I want to feel your love overtake my soul. The abundance of love that you have poured on me is like nothing I've ever experienced. All I can say is thank you, Lord. I love you with all my heart. I wouldn't trade this feeling for anything. Walk with me each day and let me feel your presence. Let your glory fall on me so that others can see your love through me. I want to be a vessel to carry your glory wherever I go. In Jesus' name, amen.

MY SCRIPTURES

Psalms 19:1-4, Exodus 33:18, 2 Corinthians 3:18, Romans 11:36, 2 Corinthians 5:9

MY CHALLENGE: WEEK 44

Oh how beautiful is the glory of God! It shouldn't be a challenge to desire His presence and to witness His glory for yourself. This week let's spend some special time with the Lord.

By now you should be praying and studying the word of God daily. If not, maybe you need to start from the beginning of this book and take it more seriously. You should be at the point now where spending time with God is just as natural as breathing.

Your assignment this week is to have a deeper, more intimate prayer time. No distractions, no other appointments, nothing but you and God. Seek his presence like never before. Stay there until you can feel His glory overtake you. I want you to experience His overwhelming love rushing in like a flood. I promise your life will never be the same.

The only way to experience this is to leave ALL problems at His feet. Don't think about anything but worshipping Him. Don't ask for anything, don't bring any burdens with you. Just worship and praise Father God for who He is to you. I am so excited for you! I cannot wait for your Godly encounter! God bless you.

MY PERSONAL JOURNAL

WEEK 44

MY GOALS:

MY ACCOMPLISHMENTS:

45 ~ UNCONDITIONAL LOVE

"For the Lord is good and His love endures forever; His faithfulness continues through all generations." (Psalms 100:5)

Everyone of us wants to be cherished and loved. As human beings born in a sinful world, we aren't always reliable. Even in the best relationships, we sometimes have to step back and question our love. Things happen over time and our feelings change. We can be deeply in love until we've been cheated on or lied to. We can love someone to pieces, as long as we can see them, but when they are out of our sight, we begin to start looking for someone else to satisfy our needs. Some people love you as long as they can control you. Some people need approval from their friends or family before they decide to love you. My friend, that is not true love. That is not God's kind of love. Aren't you glad that our God loves us unconditionally?

He loved us while we were yet sinners according to Romans 5:8. And if you keep reading to verse 10, he loved us while we were His enemies. In the book of 1 John 4:8-9 it reminds us that not only is God the source of love, but He *is* love. Almighty God is omniscient (all-knowing), omnipresent (in all places), and omnipotent (all-powerful). What a combination! He alone is the ultimate power and authority to impose His goodness on you. He is not subject to any other power, so He doesn't need approval to bless you. He alone is God, and His love for you is, and always will be, unconditional. He loves the believers as well as the unbelievers. If He didn't, how do you think He saved you? You had to come to Him as a sinner at one time in order to have salvation.

As a child of God, we must learn to love others with a Godly love. It is our duty to have a compassion for the sinner. We should see them through His eyes. If you don't have that kind of love in your heart, ask God to give it to you. His greatest commandment is for us to love one another. When you walk close enough to Jesus, that love will flow onto you. There is no way you can follow that close to Him and not pick up His characteristics. As you meditate on God's love for you, even when you aren't walking uprightly before Him, consider how much more you should be willing to love others.

Walking in love isn't always going to be easy. Pray for an understanding heart. Put yourself in the place of a lost sinner and realize how much they need God in their life. Allow His love to flow through you and His glory to draw others to Him. Isn't it a blessing to have the unconditional love of Father God covering you? Won't you share that love with someone else today?

MY PRAYER: WEEK 45

Heavenly Father, thank you for your unconditional love for me. I know that I don't deserve the unchanging love that you give. There are times when I don't even like myself, but you love me still. I may not be able to trust the love of others, but Lord I know in my heart that your love will never change, and for this I am so grateful. Help me to be more like you. Help me to allow your love to flow from my heart, even when people mistreat me, lie on me, steal from me, or ignore me. I know that all these things have been done to Jesus, but your love still remained. Forgive me for the times I didn't show Godly love and give me strength to do better. In Jesus' name I pray, amen.

MY SCRIPTURES

Psalms Chapter 100, Romans 8:35-37,
1 Peter 4:8

MY CHALLENGE: WEEK 45

Loving God is so easy to do. Learning to allow His kind of love to work in our lives towards others can be a challenge sometimes. If we learn to look at others through His eyes, we may be more compassionate about the needs of others.

This week let's focus on allowing God's unconditional love to work in our lives. We all know someone who is just hard to love sometimes. Do something kind for them. Don't look at them through your hurt or anger. You should see them as God does. We all want to be loved by someone. You are the perfect person to allow the love of God to work in that "hard-to-love" person's life. Pray and ask for direction. You'd really be surprised to see how one act of love can change the atmosphere for a person living in darkness. Remember, you were once lost and in need of Godly love from someone. You may be the only hope for someone to find Jesus. Don't let a moment pass you by to help someone change their eternity.

MY PERSONAL JOURNAL

WEEK 45

MY GOALS:

MY ACCOMPLISHMENTS:

46 ~ MY PROVIDER

"Don't be anxious about anything; but in everything by prayer and supplication with thanksgiving let your requests be made known unto God...and my God will meet all your needs according to His glorious riches in Christ Jesus." (Philippians 4:16,19)

No one has to tell you that we are living in very difficult times. Life is a struggle on so many levels, and it can cause you to become anxious if your mind is not on Jesus. It's so comforting to know that as a child of God, we don't have to worry as the world worries. We serve a God who provides generously for His people. Our American currency has the slogan "In God We Trust" printed on it. How many of us can really say that and mean it? Do we trust in God, or in money?

If you study the Bible, you'll see that God provides for His people from Genesis through Revelation. Never did His people die because of lack of provision. He provides for us here on Earth and is preparing a beautiful place for us in eternity. What a generous, loving God! But do we really trust Him for our needs today? It's easy to verbally say we trust in Him when things are going smoothly in our lives, but when the storms of life come crashing against us, our faith is tested. It's during those times you want to ask, "Will God still provide?" So many have lost their faith because they felt as if God had turned away from them. When things got rough, they had to struggle in ways they never thought were possible. In some cases, they lost everything. That's when they blame God. But is it God's fault? No it's not.

The promises and blessings of God are given freely to those who are obedient to His word. Take a look at Abraham in Genesis Chapter 22. God asked him to make the greatest sacrifice known to man, the sacrifice of his son. This is where the term Jehovah Jireh came from. In verse 14 Abraham worships God using that name. It means "my provider". Abraham obeyed God and because of that great obedience, his son was spared. God provided a ram in the bush as a sacrifice to replace Isaac, the son of Abraham. Obedience leads to provision for you as well. If you find yourself in need of God's provision, that's a perfect time to seek Him. Find out what it is He it wanting you to do. It's not a bartering situation, it's God wanting to show you that He will provide if you trust in Him. How can you prove your trust in Him unless He puts you to the test? When you are between a rock and a hard place, you'll say anything to get out. But God's provision is not based on your words, it's based on obedience. 1 Samuel 15:22 tells you that obedience is better than sacrifice.

Don't wait until you're in need of God's provision to start obeying His word. This should be your daily goal. If you live a life of constant obedience, you won't find yourself in those desperate situations as often. When you do, you already know He will provide!

MY PRAYER: WEEK 46

Lord God, thank you for being my Jehovah Jireh, my provider. I am so grateful for all that you've brought me through and for all your provision in my life. Forgive me for the times when my faith is tested and I begin to lose all hope. Help my unbelief and strengthen me to hold on and trust your word. There is none like you in all the earth. No one loves me like you do. You are all powerful and almighty in my life. I just want to praise you for your goodness. I know you to be more than enough! Help be to always be obedient to your will. In Jesus' name, amen.

MY SCRIPTURES

Genesis Chapter 22, Matthew 6:31-34, 1 Timothy 6:17, Colossians 3:23-24, John 14:27

MY CHALLENGE: WEEK 46

You cannot go through this life without ever needing God to provide something for you. When you find yourself in need of God's provision, that's the time to seek Him and find out what He desires from you. Most of the time it's a very simple task. The act of giving or helping someone else in a similar situation will open doors for your blessing.

Here are some basic questions to ask yourself. They will help open doors to your provision.

- ➢ Am I being obedient to God in all areas of my life?
- ➢ Do I have a steady prayer life, or do I just pray when I need something?
- ➢ Am I being generous to those in need?
- ➢ Have I forgiven others who have wronged me?
- ➢ Do I show Godly love to others?

Disobedience, no prayer life, holding grudges, refusing to help others, and a cold heart will all block your provision from God. Make it your lifestyle to apply these five characteristics to your life daily. Pray for more understanding so that your life will be one of "no lack". God is very generous to His children, when they obey His word. Let's do everything we can to please our Father.

MY PERSONAL JOURNAL

WEEK 46

MY GOALS:

MY ACCOMPLISHMENTS:

47 ~ MORE THAN A CONQUEROR

"Who shall separate us from the love of Christ? Shall tribulation, or distress, or persecution, or famine, or nakedness, or peril, or sword? As it is written: "For your sake we are killed all day long; we are counted as sheep for the slaughter." Yet in all these things we are more than conquerors through Him who loved us." (Romans 8:35-37)

Paul was the greatest example of being a conqueror. He was stoned, beaten, jailed, and shipwrecked. He was even faced with nakedness, hunger, thirst, and cold. He faced robbers, heathens, liars, and even his own brethren. I guess you could say he was the perfect picture of possible disaster, but Paul overcame all these circumstances with victory in his heart. He wasn't just referring to his own tribulations when he wrote this scripture, he stated that "we" are more than conquerors. That means you and I can overcome just like he did. When you think of living a victorious Christian life, you may assume that means you will get *out of* impossible situations. Actually it's quite the contrary. You are already "more than a conqueror" while in the midst of these things.

The end of this reading states that you are more than a conqueror *"through Him who loved us."* Let's break it on down. That means you'd have to be separated from Christ's love in order to be defeated. If you go on into the next two verses, 38 and 39, the word says, *"For I am persuaded that neither death nor life, nor angels nor principalities nor powers, nor things present nor things to come, nor height nor depth, nor any other created thing, shall be able to separate us from the love of God which is in Christ Jesus our Lord."*

When you read over the list of things in today's text, you see all the things Paul went through. He listed them because you too will come up against some seemingly impossible situations during your Christian walk. These are not small battles, they are sent as Spiritual Warfare by the enemy and their purpose is to wipe you out and destroy you. But you can rest assured that you are already more than a conqueror because of the love of God through Jesus Christ. MORE than a conqueror. That means that when it's all over, you won't be beaten to a pulp and rendered helpless. It means you will not only have the victory, you will be able to enjoy the benefits of overcoming. We serve a mighty God! We are victorious in every battle. There is no way you can be defeated. It may get really tough at times, but you can rest in knowing the victory has already been won through Jesus. You can face any trial that comes your way with a praise in your heart. You already know how this story ends... you win! So when those storms come, I suggest you read and meditate on these scriptures and add in 1 Corinthians 15:7, *"But thanks be to God, who gives us the victory through our Lord Jesus Christ."*

MY PRAYER: WEEK 47

Father God, thank you for your love that is so strong nothing can separate me from you. No matter what I go through and how hard things get, your love is greater than all of it. I can rest assured in knowing I am a conqueror because of that love. Give me strength to endure my storm. Sometimes all I have left is my little mustard seed faith, but I know that is enough when I turn it all over to you. I walk in victory in Jesus' name, amen.

SCRIPTURES

Romans 8: 35-39, 1 Corinthians 15:7, 1 John 4:4, John 10:10

MY CHALLENGE: WEEK 47

When you think of a conqueror, you may think of someone in a great big battle. Actually you can be a conqueror in every little thing that comes up against you. It doesn't limit victory over terrible trials. Your battle may be passing a test for school, going up for a promotion at work, qualifying for a new house or apartment, overcoming a fear, etc.

This week let's look at our challenges. What are you up against? Is there something you really want to accomplish but never got up the nerve to face it head-on? Well get ready for battle. It's time for you to conquer this thing. You are a child of God and nothing can come between you and Him. Jesus Christ has won the victory so that you too are victorious! Are you ready to claim your victory? Meditate on the word of God. These scriptures are truth and should not be taken lightly. You can do this! Let's go!

MY PERSONAL JOURNAL

WEEK 47

MY GOALS:

MY ACCOMPLISHMENTS:

48 ~ WHAT IS SUCCESS?

"For I know the plans I have for you", declares the Lord, "plans to prosper you and not to harm you, plans to give you hope and a future." (Jeremiah 29:11)

How do you define success? Money, riches, expensive homes, travel, jewelry, fine dining, luxury, and power are what the world uses to classify your measure of success. God doesn't measure it that way, and if you are a child of God you shouldn't either. Sure, He wants you to prosper. The problem comes when you take your eyes off God and start putting your wealth in His place. Worldly success and Godly success are totally different. Where your heart is will determine which scale you go by.

The true measure of success is simply the ratio of talents used to talents received by God. When you use the talents that God gave you to the best of your ability, then you bring glory to Him. This causes you to mature as a Christian, to be a blessing to others, and to expand into the greatest person you can possibly be. Once you work to do that, then you are achieving success. When attaining success in a Godly way, there will be many attacks from the enemy. He will try to get your mind trapped in greed. You must focus on increasing Godliness and decreasing self fulfillment. Your talents were not given to you for self satisfaction. When you use them for the wrong purpose it's easy to find yourself drifting away from God, thus possibly killing your success.

There are warning signs to tell you that you're beginning to drift away.

- When you start measuring your success by society standards.
- When your focus in on gaining more material things than spiritual growth.
- When receiving a higher title or status supersedes cultivating your character.
- When you begin to rely on your own abilities rather than what God can do for you.

God knows that some of His children cannot handle great wealth. It will cause them to be untrustworthy and they may not enter heaven because of that. Luke 16:11 says it best, *"So if you have not been trustworthy in handling the world's wealth, who will trust you with true riches?"* You should seek to be successful in God's eyes. This means using your talents for His glory. Everyone's talent won't make them rich, but the reward in heaven will be more valuable than anything you could ever gain on this earth! Stay Kingdom minded and God will definitely take care of you.

MY PRAYER: WEEK 48

Dear Heavenly Father, thank you for the talents you have given me. I have been trying so hard to become successful according to society's standards and have not quite met that mark. Forgive me for measuring my success by anything other than your standards. Help me use my talents for your glory. Open doors of opportunity so that I may be a blessing to others through the channels you have ordained especially for me. As I grow in grace, help me to never drift away from you because of greatness and gain. Let me be the example of good stewardship so that my success will inspire others to step out on their dreams. In Jesus' name I pray, amen.

MY SCRIPTURES

1 Timothy 6:5-19, Genesis 39:2-6, Psalms 1:1-3,
Joshua 1:8, Proverbs 3:1-4, Nehemiah 1:11, Psalms 37:34,
Proverbs 2:7, 1 Samuel 18:14, 1 Kings 2:4, Proverbs 3:6,
Malachi 3:6,
Deuteronomy 8:18, Luke 16:10-11

MY CHALLENGE: WEEK 48

We all want to be successful, it's a natural desire. Seeking success in the wrong places can cause great frustration. We as children of God don't have to resort to "get rich quick" schemes. Your focus should be on utilizing your God-given talents to the best of your ability. That is how God measures your success.

If you haven't already discovered your purpose in life, I'd suggest you begin to use your talents regularly. Pray and ask for direction if you don't know where to begin. Using your talents will bring you so much joy and satisfaction. There is an old saying, "If you do what you love, you'll never have to work a day in your life." This is so true. Once you activate your talents, the Lord will constantly provide opportunities for you to use them.

This week let's use our talents more for His glory. Sharpen your skills and prepare to let your talents used to talents received ratio be acceptable to the Lord. Remember, the goal shouldn't be getting rich, it should be pleasing God. He will take care of the rest. Now let's get to work!

MY PERSONAL JOURNAL

WEEK 48

MY GOALS:

MY ACCOMPLISHMENTS:

49 ~ ALL FOR HIS GLORY

"I am the Lord; that is my name; my glory I give no other, nor my praise to carved idols." (Isaiah 42:8)

Do you know why God created you? I'm not referring to your purpose. I mean what was God's purpose in creating you? The sum of all your gifts and talents and how you use them, the way you live your life and how you affect this world is all intended to be for the glory of God. That's right. Your main purpose is to glorify Him, to reflect His glory, and proclaim it to all creation (Isaiah 43:6-7). If what you choose to do with your life does not honor God and give Him all the glory, you are robbing Him of the purpose in which you were created. Isaiah 42:8 says that God will share His glory with no one.

Can you see how His purpose and your purpose work together? You can go back and review chapter 8 of this devotional and study Your Divine Purpose again to refresh your mind about your own purpose. As we go deeper into giving God all glory, consider the fact that you alone have a special assignment that will bring God so much joy. What does it mean to glorify Him? There are four parts to glorifying God.

- Subjection - This is when you dedicate yourself completely to God. Just as the angels in heaven wait around His throne for their commission or orders, you must do it also. Make yourself available to His will. You glorify Him by obeying Him.
- Appreciation - When you exalt Him and lift Him above anything else, this shows your appreciation (see Psalms 92:8) . Thank Him for all He's done, for who He is, and for being the great I AM.

- Adoration - This is when you worship Him (Psalms 29:2). Making time to really connect to Him on a regular basis is very honorable. Just as you love to be adored by others, God love for you to adore Him. Not prayer, but worship.
- Love - When you love Him enough to share Him with the world, that is the kind of love that pierces His heart. It's like having a new boyfriend or girlfriend. They feel like you love them, but when you introduce him or her to your family and friends, that seals the deal! God wants that same kind of love from you.

As you define or redefine your purpose in life, remember that your divine purpose is to use your talents to your best ability. God's purpose in giving you those talents is to get the glory from how you choose to use them. Are you giving Him glory, or are you being glorified?

MY PRAYER: WEEK 49

Dear Heavenly Father, thank you for giving me a special purpose to use my life to glorify you. I knew that I was created for a special reason, but it's very enlightening to know that my ultimate purpose is to glorify you. Help me to always be a blessing to others in ways that lead them back to you. I would never want to take your glory in order for me to be uplifted. I am so thankful for your love and I truly adore you. Today I want to make myself completely available to your will. I want the whole world to know how much I love you. Use me for your glory in Jesus' name, amen.

MY SCRIPTURES

1 Corinthians 10:31, John 17:4, John 4:22-24,
1 Chronicles 29:10-13, Psalms 8:1

MY CHALLENGE: WEEK 49

    We've studied about our purpose and about God's glory in previous chapters. This week is basically a reminder to use your life reflecting Jesus Christ. Now is the time to take a look at your ministry, your job, hobbies, talents, and personal life. Are you using each one to give God the glory? We can always do just a little more to step out of the light and allow it to shine on Him.

    Your challenge this week will be to perfect the four parts of glorifying God in your life. Subjection - make yourself more available to do a little more for Him. Appreciation - Don't take things for granted. Instead, thank God for the things that you may easily overlook because you've grown accustomed to having them. Adoration - Spend some time worshipping like never before. Spoil Him the way you'd like to be spoiled. Tell Him why He is great, why He is almighty, etc. Love - Share Him with your loved ones, friends, and co-workers. Introduce Him as the best thing that ever happened to you!

    Shower Him with your love this week. People should see that little twinkle in your eye when you talk about Him. There should be a glow about you, just like new love...God's love is so beautiful. Let's fall in love with Him all over again. Don't you feel all fuzzy inside already?!

MY PERSONAL JOURNAL

WEEK 49

MY GOALS:

MY ACCOMPLISHMENTS:

50 ~ BLESSINGS IN GIVING BACK

"Finally, all of you, be like-minded, be sympathetic, love one another, be compassionate and humble. Do not pay evil with evil or insult with insult. On the contrary, repay evil with blessing, because to this you were called so that you may inherit a blessing." (1 Peter 3:8-9)

Isn't it wonderful to receive blessings from God? We all enjoy that, don't we? Did you know that in addition to receiving His blessings, you are in turn supposed to be a blessing to others? God never intended for you to hoard up all of your blessings to show off or boast to everyone else.

Let's take a quick look at Genesis 12:2-3. *"And I will make you a great nation, and I will bless you, and make your name great; And so you shall be a blessing; and I will bless those who bless you, And the one who curses you, I will curse. And in you, all the families of the earth will be blessed."* The calling of Abraham was a foundation of receiving blessings and then blessing others. We are descendents of Abraham, and that same principle applies to us today. "Blessed to be a blessing" is a lot more than a slogan, it's a lifestyle to the followers of Jesus Christ.

When you sacrifice for the Kingdom, God will see to it that your needs are met. You won't only be blessed in heaven, but you will be blessed in this lifetime (read Luke 18:29-30). I love the way Luke 6:38 MSG Bible tells it, *"Give away your life; you'll find life given back, but not merely given back - given back with bonus and blessing."* We serve a very generous God. You better believe when you take care of others, Father God will take very good care of you. That's just the way He does business!

Giving back is not only a blessing to the receiver, it's a blessing to you. Use your success to encourage someone else. There is a special joy you'll get deep within your soul every time you are able to bless others. Hoarding your blessings are never enjoyed as much as shared ones. Your generosity brings glory to God and it just makes Him want to bless you even more. The giving principle works in every area of life, not just finances. Giving back doesn't only consist of your money. You can be a blessing to others in any way that you have been blessed.

Remember this: If you listen to God's voice and do what He says, you will have success and be blessed. This will impact others all around you. Now is the time to adopt the attitude of being a blessing to others and giving back. You should no longer be looking for a blessing from others, but seeking out how you can be a blessing to them. Give God your praise and worship. Give more of yourself, your love, your finances, your gifts, your time, and any other blessing you have acquired. Make a difference in your home, work, community, city, state, country, and world. You have the power to bless by giving back.

MY PRAYER: WEEK 50

Father God, thank you for blessing me in so many ways. My heart leaps for joy when I am able to use my blessings to bless others. You have been so generous to me and for that I am grateful. Help me to live according to your will so that I will always be able to receive more, and in turn I can give more. Continue to give me a compassionate heart, willing to give back. I realize that the more I give, the more I am able to give. Thank you for the joy in my heart when I reflect your love by blessing others. Continue to use me in Jesus' name, amen.

MY SCRIPTURES

Luke 12:20-21, Deuteronomy 30:9, 2 Corinthians 9:8-11, Proverbs 11:25-31, Ephesians 2:10, 5:1

MY CHALLENGE: WEEK 50

As a child of God, you should feel so good when you are able to be a blessing to someone. This is something that should be done on a regular basis. It not only blesses others, it keeps God's blessings flowing through you.

This week make it your priority to find a way to bless somebody in some way... every day. You aren't doing it to be seen or to get honored before others. The purpose of blessing them is to show God's love. We can all bless someone. A smile to a broken hearted person is a blessing. A hug to someone who has been hurt is a blessing. Free blessings are in abundance! Once you catch hold of this blessing principle, you will be opening flood gates to receive even more!!

MY PERSONAL JOURNAL

WEEK 50

MY GOALS:

MY ACCOMPLISHMENTS:

51 ~ WORTH IT ALL

"And so we keep on praying for you, that our God will make you the kind of children He wants to have - will make you as good as you wish you could be! - rewarding your faith with His power. Then everyone will be praising the name of the Lord Jesus Christ because of the results they see in you; and your greatest glory will be that you belong to Him. The tender mercy of our God and of the Lord Jesus Christ has made all this possible for you." (2 Thessalonians 1:11-12 The Living Bible)

Living for Jesus will not always be easy. No one said that it would be. But if you want to be real, living in sin is a miserable way to live. Especially when you know the outcome is eternal hell. After disciplining yourself to follow this weekly devotional, I pray that you have learned the benefits of turning your life over to God and obeying His will. You must realize by now that no matter what you've sacrificed to follow Jesus, it could never out-weigh what God sacrificed for you. Not only that, you should have learned by now that your reward will be so much greater than what you left behind.

Paul prayed constantly for Christians, this scripture is an example of that. Your constant prayer should be for God to help you to overcome your sinful desires, and help you live according to the calling He has over your life. Living by faith and trusting in His word will take you far beyond anything you could ever dream for yourself. Pray for His love to be reflected in your life. All you do for the Kingdom of God is worth everything you have to go through.

Your sacrifice will never compare to God's. You are worth Jesus' death. He died for you, so you should be willing to live for Him. I pray that this book will help you strengthen your relationship with God, understand His word, and learn to hear

His voice. God has called us to serve Him by serving and encouraging others. If you have breath in your body, there is something you can do for the Lord. Step out on faith and make yourself available to Him. Only you can decide if living for Christ is worth your life of dedication to Him. Romans 12:1 says, *"And so, dear brothers and sisters, I plead with you to give your bodies to God. Let them be a living and holy sacrifice - the kind He will accept. When you think of what He has done for you, is this too much to ask?"*

Father God loves you more than you could ever understand. You are so precious to Him. Living a life that is honorable to Him would be the best gift that you could give in return. *"His divine power has given us everything we need for a Godly life through our knowledge of Him who called us by His own glory and goodness."* (2 Peter 1:3) You have the power to live a Godly life. You were created to be victorious in all you do. It's worth it all!

MY PRAYER: WEEK 51

Father God, today I want to thank you from the bottom of my heart for your sacrifice of Jesus Christ. It is through that sacrifice that I have been redeemed of all sin in my life. It is because of that sacrifice that I can claim my right as an heir to your Kingdom. I could never sacrifice anything that would compare to what you've done for me. I offer my life to you. I will let your love shine through me so that others can see how much you love them. Lord, I am honored to be your child. Thank you for giving me the power to overcome anything that tries to hinder me in this journey. Let my life be encouragement to others. Let the work I do be used to glorify you. In Jesus' name, amen.

MY SCRIPTURES

Psalms 119:33-40, 1 Corinthians 15:58,
Ecclesiastes 9:10, Ephesians 6:7

MY CHALLENGE: WEEK 51

Dedication to God is honorable before Him. It's way more than a verbal acceptance of Jesus. True dedication to Him means turning your life completely over to Him in all you do. Sometimes it can be easy to become complacent in our daily walk. We get comfortable in knowing that we are His children and that we are on our way to heaven one day. When that happens, we slack off on Kingdom assignments.

This week let's re-dedicate our lives to Him. Let's start fresh in our relationship. Worship Him, praise Him, love Him like never before. We need to rekindle the fire in our hearts again so that there is no room for complacency. Ask God to give you a fresh anointing to do even greater things for the Kingdom.

There is so much to be done, but there are too many "bench warmers" sitting in the church. We need more team players, more willing workers, and more fisherman to bring in the lost and needy. What can you do differently to encourage others to come to Jesus? How can you reflect Jesus from your heart into this dying world? Your challenge is to re-dedicate your devotion to Him. Your heart should say, "open availability".

MY PERSONAL JOURNAL

WEEK 51

MY GOALS:

MY ACCOMPLISHMENTS:

52 ~ HIS PEARL I AM

"Therefore, since we have been justified through faith, we have peace with God through our Lord Jesus Christ, through we have gained access by faith into His grace in which we now stand. And we boast in the hope of the glory of God. Not only so, but we also glory in our sufferings, because we know that sufferings produces perseverance; perseverance, character; and character, hope. And hope does not put us to shame, because God's love has been poured out into our hearts through the Holy Spirit, who has been given to us." (Romans 5:1-5)

In the beginning of this book, I shared with you the story of how the pearl is created. After going through each devotion, you can now compare your own life to that of a pearl. Sure, it has great value. But look at all it had to endure before that value could be cherished. That's exactly how your life can be described. You are His pearl. You are so valuable, not because of what you are now, but because of all you had to go through to get to this beautiful stage.

Today's scripture refers to "glory in sufferings". Just as the glory of God could be seen in the cross, His glory can be seen in all your sufferings as well. God sees beyond all the pain and suffering right to the true value of His pearls. It's through your tribulations that your true character is revealed. The pearl is created because of a grain of sand or an irritant enters its shell. Your irritants are the things you have to endure. You didn't volunteer to have them. Your irritant may be a terminal illness, a divorce, the loss of a family member, or any great tragedy. God uses those things to bring beauty out of you. The way you bounced back even stronger than before. The way you didn't crumble under the pressure. Your divine strength and faith in God caused others to look at you with great admiration. What should have killed you only made you better! THIS is what increased your value.

When you go through trials with grace instead of grumpiness, you reflect God's character and strength. The more you allow Him to be revealed in times of crisis, the more Godly beauty is revealed in yourself. You are His pearl. You are worth far more than anyone could ever imagine. All because you were able to stand firm and allow the process to run its course. We are all a work in progress. We weren't instantly made into a perfect jewel. We must all go through the process. Your great value is honored in the eyes of God because only He knows every detail of your story. He knows about each layer that went into the making of His pearls. You are being admired by people you thought never noticed you. They saw you overcome, and now they stand in awe. You have now been formed into a timeless jewel. You can proudly say, "HIS PEARL I AM!"

MY PRAYER: WEEK 52

Dear Father God, thank you for being with me through every storm and trial in my life. I realize that all I've gone through has given me more strength, knowledge, and power. All that I've endured has increased my love for you and my value in your eyes. My life is not over, and I know that there will be more layers added to it. Thank you for giving me the grace to continue this process. I praise you for each layer of becoming your beautiful pearl. Help me to accept the process of my progress. May all that I go through bring more glory and honor to you. Help the beauty of my life enhance your Kingdom. I am your pearl. I am worth far more than the human eye can see. I praise you! In Jesus' name, amen.

MY SCRIPTURES

Romans 5:2-8, Luke 12:6-7, Psalms 103:14,
1 Corinthians 7:23, Exodus 19:5, 1 Peter 1:18-19,
Isaiah 43:1-4, Psalms 50:2, Ecclesiastes 3:11,
Psalms 139:13

MY CHALLENGE: WEEK 52

The pearl is one of the world's most precious gems. Although it turns out beautifully, the process is anything but fabulous. The same can be said about us. We know that all things work together for good for those who love God and are called according to His purpose (Romans 8:28), but the process of "all things" working together consists of a LOT of tribulations and challenges.

This week let's take some time to remember all we have survived, overcome, and conquered to get to this point in our lives. It's good to reflect on where you've come from in order to increase your faith for where you are going. You're a pearl in your own right, but God is not finished with you yet. Your story is not over. He still has some touching up to do on you.

Thank Him for your journey thus far and prepare yourself for greater. There is so much more waiting for you. When you look back at the things God has done, it should encourage you for what lies ahead. If He did it then, He will do it again..plus some more! Your past is fuel for your future. Give it all you've got, and watch God do the rest. You are a testimony in the making. Continue on, go forth in faith. You were created for greatness!

MY PERSONAL JOURNAL

WEEK 52

MY GOALS:

MY ACCOMPLISHMENTS:

CONCLUSION

The past 52 weeks have been amazing! You have successfully built a stronger relationship with Father God. Not only that, you've discovered so much more about yourself. Living a life that gives God glory is why you were created. Being showered with His favor and blessings are the benefits. In order to maintain a healthy Christian life that is acceptable to God, you should always:

- Pray daily, preferably more than once a day. Pray for guidance, tell Him your problems and concerns, thank Him for what He's done and who He is, and pray for others.
- Read and study the word. This is your instruction manual. Psalms 119:18 says *"Open my eyes to see the wonderful truths in your law."* Ask God to reveal His word to you.
- Allow the Holy Spirit, who lives within your heart, to direct you daily. He will give you strength and guidance right when you need it. He will comfort you at all times.
- Attend a bible teaching church regularly. You need to stay spiritually fed. You also find strength in being around other believers. Also open yourself up to staying busy in your church.
- Serve others. The more you give of yourself to help others, the more you will enjoy your Christian life.
- Take one day at a time. Your past is gone, you can't change it. Tomorrow is not promised to you. All you have is now. Do all you can to live like Christ today.
- Tell others about Jesus. Share your testimony with others.

When you are in the presence of others, they should feel good when you walk away. Never try to force your church or religion on anyone. But tell them in a loving way where your joy comes from. Offer to pray for them. Be a true friend. Live a Godly life everywhere you go. People are watching what you do and how you do it. Your best way to win souls for Christ is to live what you teach. You may be the first bible they read!

Your devotion to God is very important. Now that you've developed a stronger relationship with Him, continue to get even closer. The more you are in His presence, the more powerful you become. You can never get too much of Him. He is a well that never runs dry. Your hunger for Him should increase daily. Congratulations on becoming even better, stronger, and wiser than you were a year ago. May God continue to bless you.

MINISTRY ACKNOWLEDGMENTS

THE BRIDGE CHURCH
Pastors Bill and Debbie Bryan
334-742-0144
www.thebridge.ws

REVIVAL NOW MINISTRIES
Evangelist David Copeland
www.revivalnow.org

SWORD DRAWN MINISTRIES
Evangelist Anthony Cole
www.sworddrawnministries.org

SOAR MINISTRY
Evangelist Eusherla Pitts
email: soarministry@gmail.com
334-610-1704
Facebook: SOAR Ministry
Twitter: @SOARMinistry

THE BRIDGE CHURCH - Chipley, FL
Pastors Tony and Rhonda Hagan
850-773-1111
www.TheBridgeatSunnyhills.com

All of these ministries have been a great blessing to me. If you're ever in need of Spiritual guidance, special prayer, or want to sow a seed into their ministries feel free to contact them. God bless you!

ABOUT THE AUTHOR

Sharon Fox was born in Tennessee, raised in Indiana, and now divides her time between the southern living of Alabama and the Alamo City of San Antonio, Texas. She was always a very peculiar child, learning to talk to God in her own special way and imagining to actually sit on His lap and lay in His arms.

Sharon has been known for profoundly inspiring and encouraging people from all over the world for over thirty years. She has mentored many young people, participated in several homeless ministries, volunteered in many community education events, and comforted the hearts of countless others. Sharon is the author of two previous cookbooks.

For the past eight years, she's touched many hearts through written word and devotions. After much prayer and seeking God, she has answered the call to devote her life to writing inspirational literature. Her practical approach to applying scriptures for facing and overcoming life's obstacles is nothing less than amazing. The anointing on her life can be felt through each page of her work. *HIS PEARL I AM* is the first in her series of Christian publications.

Today Sharon enjoys baking cookies and treats for the homeless or donating them to hospital I.C.U. waiting rooms. When she isn't glued to a computer screen, she spends time reading or enjoying her sons and grandchildren. Sharon loves her church and enjoys writing devotions for their social media pages. Above all, Sharon loves the Lord with all her heart. She has a secret desire to learn to play the harp…only for God. You can contact Sharon by email at: AuthorSharonFox@gmail.com.

www.ingramcontent.com/pod-product-compliance
Lightning Source LLC
Chambersburg PA
CBHW071855290426
44110CB00013B/1158